CREED *of* LOVE

REFLECTIONS ON THE APOSTLES' CREED

'These are recorded so that you may believe that Jesus is the Christ, the Son of God, and that believing this you may have life through his name.'

(John 20:31)

Billy Swan

VERITAS

First published 2006 by
Veritas Publications
7/8 Lower Abbey Street
Dublin 1
Ireland
Email publications@veritas.ie
Website www.veritas.ie

ISBN 1 85390 977 7

A catalogue record for this book
is available from the British Library.

Printed in the Republic of Ireland
by Betaprint Dublin

Veritas books are printed on paper made from the wood pulp of managed
forests. For every tree felled, at least one tree is planted, thereby renewing
natural resources.

To the People of the Diocese of Ferns

ACKNOWLEDGEMENTS

I would like to thank the following people for their encouragement in writing this book:

To my family, friends and colleagues for their constant presence and support. To the staff and my fellow students at the Pontifical Irish College, Rome, where this manuscript was completed. To all the staff at Veritas Publications, for their time and patience as this work was being prepared. To Bishop Brendan Comiskey and Bishop Eamonn Walsh.

Finally, to all who have inspired this book by the faith you share, I sincerely thank you. It would be impossible to mention everyone by name and so my hope is that you will recognise something of your life in what I have written: that you may recognise your story in His story and His story in your story.

Scripture quotations are taken from *The New Jerusalem Bible*, London: Darton, Longman & Todd, 1990.

Contents

PART I

INVITED TO FAITH

INTRODUCTION

I remember once meeting a man in the parish at a reception having celebrated the funeral Mass of his mother. After chatting for a while, he began to share some of the questions that had arisen in his heart with this loss in his life. Concerning his faith, he said, 'I want to believe in something, but I don't always know what to believe in. I have always believed in God since I was a child, but with my mother's death, there is much confusion and doubt'. On hearing this, my mind was cast back to the Gospel incident when the father of a young boy possessed by an evil spirit approached Jesus and spoke those words that we all can make our own, 'Lord, I believe, help my unbelief!' (Mark 9:24).

I think many of us can sympathise with this man's plight. We all find ourselves a little lost sometimes and perhaps a little confused as to where our lives are going and indeed what life is all about. Who am I? What does my life mean? Where have I come from? What is my destiny? I think the friend I met that day is typical of many of us who do believe but who find that the simple faith of our childhood, though still present, is unable to shed sufficient light on the deeper questions that an adult's life experience throws up. For many of us there is a gap that exists between our faith and the complexity of our life experience. How can one speak to the other? What exactly is our faith saying or offering to us? What does it mean?

Creed of Love takes up the challenge to explore the meaning and significance of the Apostles' Creed, which is a summary of what the Church believes. It aims to clarify what it is we actually believe in order to rediscover and appreciate the precious gift of faith and find meaning in it for our lives. My prayer is that it helps unpack the riches and beauty of our Christian faith that we have been blessed with and perhaps the significance of which we are unaware. In the early Church, the Creed was a summary of how people experienced the mystery of God in their lives. It was born from their experience of an encounter with the living God. Here the aim is to go in the opposite direction, beginning with the Creed and teasing out how it connects with our experience of life as we find it today. My hope is that it helps people like my friend who had lost his mother to discover fresh hope and meaning in a life that is a wonderful adventure and joy once it is lived in God. Those who yearn for the Spirit of love, the Spirit of God, will feel her fire as they begin to understand her. I hope that with these words, God may speak something more of his everlasting love for us, a love that is beyond our wildest imagination and that is forever reaching out to us at every moment of every day.

WHERE TO BEGIN:
GOD LOVED US FIRST

Introduction

Before we come to look at the Apostles' Creed let us remind ourselves of what exactly gives birth to faith in God. We need to reflect on what inspires it, namely a human person's experience of the love of God. We continue to bear in mind that faith is a response to an initiative of God to reveal himself to individuals and communities. Therefore it seems like a good idea to build these reflections of faith on the solid foundation of God's revealed love for humanity. This love is like a glorious light that shines through everything we believe in and hold to be true and beautiful including all the teachings, doctrines, creeds, spirituality, sacraments and preaching of the Church. They are all part of the great drama that is the love story between God and his people.

Our Search for God

One of the most sacred human experiences we can have is that of falling in love with another human being. People have described it as finding in the other the one they had been searching for all their lives. Friends may look on and describe a couple as being 'made for each other'. Their love consumes their minds in a way that they can think of nothing else but the other. Two lovers thinking about each other; two lovers wanting each other; here is a good starting point for our reflection on the truth that we were made for God and that he invites us to be madly in love with him as he is with us.

Deep inside each of us is a desire to question, to search and to wonder. We can speak of our search for God because of the way we find our human nature. There is a deep longing, a hunger and a restlessness that is part of who we are. It is a hunger that has been in the heart of humanity since the very beginning for 'He has put eternity into man's mind' (Ecclesiastes 3:11). The psalms appeal to us because they express beautifully what we experience to be true, 'O God, you are my God, for you I long; for you my soul is thirsting. My body pines for you like a dry, weary land without water' (Psalm 62).

We hunger for beauty, love, intimacy, the truth. Indeed all human activity is related to our search, wittingly or unwittingly, for total truth and total happiness that can only be found in God. Our searching is only a response to an initiative that comes from elsewhere; we would not be seeking God unless he was seeking us first. He wants us to find him for his delight is to be with us always. In the depths of our being he is drawing us to seek him more persistently as life goes on. It is a search that has a happy ending. Our desires have an achievable goal, namely that of total union with God who is the fullness of beauty, of love, of intimacy and truth. As Jesus promises us, 'No one who drinks the water that I shall give will ever be thirsty again: the water that I shall give will become a spring of water within, welling up for eternal life' (John 4:14). It is like God has created us in such a way as to draw us to himself. St Augustine put it well when he described his own search for God that had taken him on many paths: 'You have made us for yourself O God and our hearts are restless until they rest in thee!'[1]

---

1   *Confessions,* Book 1,1; 10, 27.

Prayer:

'O Lord, teach me to seek you, and reveal yourself to me as I seek, because I can neither seek you if you do not teach me how, nor find you unless you reveal yourself. Let me seek you in desiring you; let me desire you in seeking you; let me find you in loving you; let me love you in finding you.'[2]

God's Search for us

In the Book of Genesis, the story is told of Adam and Eve in the Garden of Eden and how they disobeyed the command of God by eating the fruit of the tree. We are told that once they realised their sin they felt shame before each other, fled the scene and hid in the long grass. The story then tells us something very interesting about God's approach. He does not threaten or destroy but rather he pursued humanity 'in the cool of the day' (cf. Gen. 3:8), asking the question, 'Where are you?'

Having found them he offered them another chance to share his divine love. This initiative of God was a sign of things to come throughout the Old Testament and continued in the New Testament with Jesus. The Bible recalls many stories from the history of our Jewish ancestors and the history of the Christian community we call the Church. There is a constant theme running throughout: that of God's love for his people and his saving presence in their history. It is a love story that is marked by intimacy, love, betrayal, separation, reconciliation and forgiveness.

---

2   St Anselm of Canterbury. From *The Proslogion of St Anselm*, Chapter 1.

In the New Testament, the love of God for his people is revealed in a new and deeper way. In the Old Testament, God searched for his people but now through his Son Jesus he showed us how far he was prepared to go in order to find them and be with them. Jesus gathers people into a family and includes those who previously were excluded. He is the Good Shepherd who pursues the lost sheep even to the remotest places and who does not rest until he has safely returned it to the flock (cf. Luke 15). At the Eucharist, we recall the nature of God's mercy that never gives up on us, 'Even when we disobeyed you and lost your friendship you did not abandon us to the power of death but helped all people to seek and to find you' (Eucharistic Prayer IV).

As he was dying on the cross, Jesus uttered the words 'I thirst' (John 19:28). His thirst was a severe physical thirst because of dehydration and loss of blood but his words also have a deeper spiritual meaning in terms of God's thirst for us. He thirsts for us to live the fullness of life that he came to offer and so be living witnesses to the glory of God. He thirsts for our recognition and our affection. At the side of a well near Galilee, Jesus addressed us through the Samaritan woman when he said 'Give me something to drink' (John 4:7). What a question! With these words, Jesus shows how he had 'taken the form of a slave' (cf. Philippians 2:7) and asks for our love like a someone hungry asks for bread. Before he died, Jesus prays 'Father, I want those you have given me to be with me where I am' (John 17:24). These words reveal a man and a God who longs for the company of those he loves so dearly. And so we see that we thirst for God but that God also thirsts for us.

It is a beautiful thought to think of God as our lover. Just like a lover, he wants to be with us, he wants our attention, wants to listen to us and to hear our voice. St Paul tells us that 'No eye has seen nor ear heard, things beyond the mind of humans, has

God prepared for those who love Him' (1 Corinthians 2:9). Such a statement gives us a tiny insight into the wonder of who we are as God's children. The human love we share between us is but a glimpse of God's love but is never equal to it. God promises us that the best is yet to come.

Prayer:

> *'Father, I abandon myself into your hands, do with me what you will.*
> *Whatever you may do, I thank you: I am ready for all, I accept all.*
> *Let only your will be done in me and in all your creatures.*
> *I wish no more than this, O Lord.*
> *Into your hands, I commend my soul;*
> *I offer it to you with all the love of my heart;*
> *For I love you, Lord,*
> *And so need to give myself:*
> *To surrender myself into your hands without reserve and with boundless confidence:*
> *For you are my Father.'*[3]

God is Love

There was a time when the prospect of listening to a homily on the topic of God's unconditional love would not have particularly excited me. For me and others at that time it was not what was needed. What was required in our view was more of a 'get tough' attitude that included a well worked-out strategy aimed at 'getting people back' to the Church and their

---

3   Charles de Foucauld, Prayer of Abandonment.

faith. Looking back at this time in my life, I approach God with a deep sense of humility and repentance for my flawed vision of how things should be. Sure, I believed that God loved me but it was a dry and academic belief. I believed with my head but the message had yet to sink in to my heart. I had yet to make the connection between my belief in the love of God and how the evidence of it filled my day. I could not see what Thomas Merton saw as the gate of heaven being everywhere. This brings us back to the basic question of just where do we begin in this process of sharing the Good News with everyone and growing together in faith. What is our starting point?

When looking for the answer to this question, we are grateful to St John for pointing us in the right direction. Writing a letter to a community of early Christians, John brings them back to basics and reminds them about what the Christian faith is all about. 'God loved us first' (1 John 4:10) is a simple statement but it means that ever before the human race existed, the love of God was always there. Before we were old enough to do or say anything, God's love smiled on us. The 'Good News' is news of the truth that the gift of God's love is offered to us freely at every moment of every day. He is our creator whose spirit fills our life and is ever present to us. The birth of faith that is genuine and sincere comes as a response to the experience of love that is an experience of God. It is as if the love of God that shines on us brings out the same love that is within, as with a mother and child: 'After a mother has smiled for a long time at her child, the child will begin to smile back; she has awakened love in its heart, and in awakening love in its heart, she awakens recognition as well. In the same way, God explains himself before us as love. Love radiates from God and instils the light of love in our hearts.'[4]

---

4   Hans Urs Von Balthasar, *Love Alone is Credible*, San Francisco: Ignatius Press, 2005, Chapter 5.

Let us take a look at the example of St Paul who was a great missioner for Christ. As a witness and preacher of God's love, he was successful in his preaching with the birth and foundation of many Christian communities. As we know, St Paul used to be a persecutor of the Church who co-operated in the death of many Christians including St Stephen, the first martyr (cf. Acts 7:58). Following his conversion on the way to Damascus (cf. Acts 9:1ff), we are told that Paul understandably had some trouble being accepted by some of the Churches because of his reputation as a persecutor of the Church. Paul was aware of this but never denied his dark and controversial past. Instead he pointed to himself as the best witness to the mercy and love of God because he had been the greatest sinner (cf. Acts 9:26). He is open and frank about his past and how mercy was shown him: 'I used to be a blasphemer and a persecutor and contemptuous. Mercy however was shown me' (1 Timothy 1:13). From then on, Paul could not be kept silent about the mercy of the Lord that he had experienced first hand, even being glad in suffering humiliation as a consequence. He was a first-hand witness to the love of God that is prepared to go to great lengths to offer itself to those most in need of it. Wherever he travelled Paul met with audiences who were well versed in philosophy and theology, people who were more educated than he was. Not only that but he carried the Christian message to cultures of paganism and to people who had never even heard of God. For Paul, his starting point was not a cleverly worked-out argument or strategy. For him, all he preached was 'Jesus Christ and him crucified' (1 Corinthians 2:2). The secret of his success lay in the fact that 'the Lord stood by me and gave me power so that through me the message might be fully proclaimed' (2 Timothy 4:17). Paul delighted in sharing the news about God's love and how it had become a real experience in his life. In fact he was so moved by the love of Jesus that he could say, 'Indeed I count everything as loss because of the surpassing worth of knowing Christ Jesus' (Philippians 3:8). The God of Paul was not an abstraction or a distant, uncaring and impersonal power. Would he have been happy to suffer beatings and torture as he did for a god like this? Who would? Paul endured his suffering because he had finally found the 'pearl of great value' (Matthew 13:46), the 'one thing needful' (Luke 10:42). Because of it, he was 'anxious for nothing' (Matthew 6:25-34). For Paul, 'God is love' (1 John 4:8) was the point of it all, was the centre, was everything. As St Teresa of Avila wrote about him: 'It seems he [Paul] could do no other than speak about Jesus continually because he had Jesus so engraved and printed upon his heart.'[5] Paul's preaching generated excitement in himself and in those around him. He burned with zeal to communicate this message of God's love and truth that was fully revealed to humanity when Jesus gave his life for us on the cross. His success as a preacher depended far more on the inspiration of the Holy Spirit than on his own skills or ability. He could not keep the Good News to himself but felt impelled to tell everyone about Jesus crucified and risen.

The fruits of Paul's labours were the birth of faith and the spread of the Church. Those who came to believe in Jesus did so as a response to the Word of God that Paul was sharing. It was a spoken word and a lived word, spoken by those who lived the message they shared. Today, as we find ourselves in challenging times, we would do well to learn from St Paul and build upon the rock of God's revealed love for the world and for every human person. Love inspires faith and a real experience of God compels us to share it with others and to express that

---

5   St Teresa of Avila, *The Collected Works of St Teresa of Avila*, Vol. 1, Washington DC: ICS Publications, 1987, Chapter 22.

love concretely in lives of service. It is not by accident that the Creed comes after the homily in the order of Mass. Sharing the Good News of God's love in the homily based on the Gospel or the readings is followed by us standing with hearts renewed and faith nourished, responding with our whole being to what we have just heard with the words 'I believe ...'.

Prayer:

'O Lord my God, I do not want only to hear about your love. I want to know it! Like St Paul, may your love and truth burn in my heart so that I may help spread faith in you as he did. Amen.'

FAITH: OUR RESPONSE TO GOD

Believing in his Love

Pause for a moment and recall a time in your life when you saw signs of someone's affection and genuine goodness towards you. Perhaps it was the way that someone looked at you and smiled, a gift they bought you, the way they thanked you, encouraged you, spoke well of you: one of those moments that come around once in a while when we are confronted by the goodness of another in a way that affirms the presence of the good in us. We walk taller when this happens, with an extra spring in our step.

Such is the effect of believing that we are loved by God. Faith such as this inspires goodness in those around us without diminishing itself. It is like a candle that lights another without losing anything of its own brightness. Before too long there is a fire that spreads and changes the world. We have seen how God's love for humankind is the starting point for the birth of genuine faith. This is a reminder to us of the importance of all Christians being people of mission who are prepared to carry God's love into the world. Coming to know the love of God at first hand inspires us to go out and introduce others to that experience. Very few today are interested in a second-hand God or being told of a God that only others have experienced. People are only interested in a God that they too can experience as real. True people of faith are those who have experienced the saving love of God in their own lives and who want to share it with the whole world. Becoming aware of the everlasting gaze of God's love, inspires us in turn to love in the same way. The love of another awakens us to respond and calls us to trust. Believing that God loves us with our head may take only a few seconds. Believing it with our hearts takes a lifetime.

Taking a chance on God loving us requires a great deal of trust. A barrier to the growth of faith today is a reluctance on our part to trust. When we look back on our life experience, there may be good reasons why this is the case. The sad reality is that we can't always assume that everyone is on our side and will act with our interest at heart. Few things hurt more than a trust that has been betrayed and few things are more damaging to faith in humanity and God. Our Church is still recovering from the shocking revelations of child abuse committed by a number of priests and the pain that their sins have caused. The victims tell the story of their suffering and of the betrayal of trust that is so hard to bear. In some cases the victims tell of how their capacity to trust anyone again has been destroyed and how their faith in God and Church has evaporated. Yet, the Lord asks us to 'trust in God still and trust in me' (John 14:1). He invites us to trust that he is totally on our side and is only interested in what is best for us. The trust that we invest in him will never be betrayed: 'We may be unfaithful but God is always faithful for he cannot disown his own self' (2 Timothy 2:13). This is the faith that is the master key and that unlocks all the doors of our life to God's presence and power. Jesus invites us to trust in God and to place ourselves into his hands as he has placed himself in ours. Believing is making the decision, assisted and prompted by his grace, to take a chance and trust in him.

It is interesting to see from the Bible how sin entered into the world. Adam and Eve fell to the temptations of the serpent who lured them into doubting that God knew what was best for them and introduced a suspicion that God cannot be trusted, 'No! You will not die. God knows in fact that the day you eat it [the fruit of the tree] your eyes will be opened and you will be like gods, knowing good from evil' (Genesis 3:4). Sin sets up our will in opposition to that of God's will. It entices us to trust no one but ourselves and to 'go it alone'. True faith helps us trust that God wants only the best for those he loves.

The Bible holds up Abraham as our Father of faith in the Old Testament and Mary as the model of faith in the New Testament. Both people had total obedience, trust and faith in the God they believed was totally on their side. Abraham was asked to sacrifice his only son Isaac and still trust that God was acting in his best interests (cf. Genesis 22:1-14). In the midst of suffering we may be tempted to give up on the notion of God's goodness towards us. But as in the case of Abraham, our faith helps us see beyond the present experience and to trust that God always acts with our long-term good in mind.

The same is true in the case of Mary. At the Annunciation she accepted God at his word, 'let what you have said be done to me' (Luke 1:38). Knowing how her life unfolded, we imagine that there must have been many times when she was tempted to believe that she had been deceived. She may have asked herself at the foot of the cross, 'How could a God who only wants my good and happiness have led me to this hell?' But such was the depth of her faith that she never gave up on God's promises that 'He made to our ancestors, of his mercy to Abraham and to his descendants forever' (Luke 1:55). As a descendent of Abraham, she believed that just as God did not deceive Abraham, he would not deceive her either. Like Abraham she is truly blessed because she believed that 'The promise made to her by the Lord would be fulfilled' (Luke 1:45).

Such perfect faith is a goal that we strive for. God's grace is at work in us all the time and our faith is constantly growing in response to our life experiences. The response of faith to the love of God in our lives will vary from person to person. Each of us will respond according to what we are capable of and to what we have been given: 'When someone is entrusted with a great deal, of that person even more will be expected' (Luke 12:48). Only God can judge the extent of our generosity as we respond to what he has revealed. Our response can never be equal to God's initiative. Every time we say 'yes' to God he invites us forward into another set of circumstances where we will be asked to respond again. Perhaps it is like Peter, who was asked three times to affirm his love for Jesus after the resurrection (cf. John 21). Our faith is changing and maturing as we live. Our 'yes' to God is asked of us every day. Faith is our personal adherence to a God who reaches out to us in love and who has revealed himself in Jesus Christ. Through the presence of Jesus in the community of believers, God is forever inviting us into a deeper relationship with him. The capacity to believe and to take a chance on God loving us, comes as a gift of the Holy Spirit who makes it easy for us to accept and believe the truth. The Holy Spirit assists us to say the final 'yes' to God that he invites us to make. This is what we call faith. It is our 'yes' to God's 'yes' that comes first.

Finally, our faith is free. No one can be forced to believe against their will. Jesus invited people to faith but never forced them. His was an invitation of 'Come and see' (John 1:39). In this sense, making an act of faith is always an act of freedom and choice, for God can do all things except force a human being to love him in return. The Lord remains outside the door of our hearts. He knocks and waits patiently for us to open (cf. Revelation 3:20).

Prayer:

'God our Father, through Jesus your Son, you ask us to trust you. Help us to overcome our fears and to believe that your love is true and genuine. Help us believe like Abraham and Mary that your love will never let us down and remains with us always. At times of doubt and difficulty, be with us and increase our trust in you. Send your healing Spirit upon all those whose trust in someone has been betrayed. May they find healing and hope in Jesus who was himself betrayed by a friend. May we learn to forgive ourselves and others as you have forgiven us. Amen.'

Doubt

Having faith does not mean that we are strangers to doubt. Indeed doubt can be the instrument that purifies our faith. None of us should be surprised if we find ourselves struggling with doubt in the course of our lives of faith. Many things that are part of our experience put the strongest faith to the test. The world can seem like a very dark and frightening place at times because of evil and suffering. Yet it is the gift of faith that gives us the hope to carry on and to believe that bad things do not have the final say. In spite of darkness, we respond with hope and not despair.

St Therese of Lisieux was a person who was no stranger to doubt. It would be wrong to think that this great saint always felt close to God. On the contrary she wrote: 'God permitted my soul to be invaded by the thickest darkness, and the thought of heaven, until then so sweet to me, became the cause of struggle and torment. This trial was to last not a few days or a few weeks, it was not to be extinguished until the hour set by God himself.'[1]

Despite her darkness and persistent doubts, Therese persevered in faith along her journey and clung to her conviction that God was near even though she could not feel his presence. Without sensing God's intimacy, Therese could say, 'I believe I have made more acts of faith in this past year than all through my whole life. At each new occasion of combat ... I run towards my Jesus'.[2]

May St Therese and all the other men and women of honest struggle pray for us that we may make a generous response of faith to God and live that faith with sincerity and courage.

Prayer:

'O Lord I believe, help my unbelief! You know my heart, Lord, you know me through and through. You know my doubts and my struggle to believe in you. In the middle of my darkness and confusion, where are you? In the middle of famine and disaster, where are you? In my restlessness, in my longing I want to believe and hope. I want to know that there is a point to it all. Yet sometimes it seems to get harder. In spite of everything, help me to find you and to trust that you are here with me even when I cannot feel you are close. Lord I believe! Help the little faith I have! Amen.'

---

1   St Therese of Lisieux, *Story of a Soul: The Autobiography of St Therese of Lisieux, General Correspondence,* Manuscript C, p. 211, J. Clarke (ed.), Washington DC: ICS, 1996.

2   Ibid, p. 213.

Happy to be Me!

Believing that we are loved unconditionally by God and that such is this love that he gave up his own Son for us provides us with a security in our own identity. It empowers us to be happy in our own skin. The infinite and personal love he bears towards each one of us speaks of our uniqueness and affirms that when he created us, God already knew everything about us: 'Before I formed you in the womb I knew you; before you came to birth I consecrated you' (Jeremiah 1:5). When we are aware of his love, we do not want to be anyone else. Because God knows us better than we know ourselves, it is only by staying close to God that we come to know who we truly are and come to love in ourselves what God sees and loves in us. Our relationship with God in faith becomes the rock of our identity as people. Once again, we need look no further than the Lord's example for this. For Jesus, his relationship with his Father was the bedrock of his life. It inspired his every thought word and deed. He knew what he was about, namely his Father's kingdom, and he would not rest or be swayed until he had accomplished the work the Father had sent him to do. The temptations of the Devil as recorded in Matthew's Gospel (cf. 4:1ff) portray this, as does his passion. He could have saved himself had he abandoned his mission to bear witness to the Father and to the truth. His acute awareness of the Father's love and the compassion that burned in his heart helped him overcome fear of anyone or anything, except his impending death in Gethsemane. We are told in the Scriptures that his teaching made a deep impression on people because he taught them with authority. This was because he was free to speak the truth despite how unpopular it was going to be. Neither praise nor criticism controlled him. His love helped him overcome any desire to take from others instead of giving to them. He knew that his happiness depended not on what he had but on who he was, namely the Son of his Father. For this reason, he did not cling to people or form possessive relationships, but moved from place to place, even when his ministry was being successful in a given community (cf. Mark 1:38).

I think it is fair to say that, in our human weakness, all of us are prone to insecurity. When we take our eyes off God's lavish and undeserved love for us, we run the danger of becoming caught up in ourselves and becoming more insecure and selfish. We may feel threatened by others we know who have more than us or who seem to be better able to compete in life than we are. We may feel envious of those whom we feel are more attractive to the opposite sex, more talented than us or who do not have to work as hard as we do. We may be afraid of being left alone in life and so may adjust our personalities and true uniqueness in order to enter into relationships that are not built on love and mutual respect. We may go to extremes to avoid being perceived as people who crave affection, acceptance and love. If we have doubts that God loves us we can end up trying to constantly prove that we are loved and accepted by others. We can easily end up controlling a relationship for our own ends rather than giving freely for the good of the other person.

The truth of God's love for us is a message of Good News that frees us from all this baggage. It was for this reason that Jesus came 'To bring good news to the poor, to proclaim liberty to captives and sight to the blind' (Luke 4:18-19). It unburdens us and makes our journey through life more joyful and happy. It assures us that no matter how life goes for us, God's love will never change and will always be there. It allows us to love freely without looking for payback and to give freely without the tag attached that says 'You owe me'.

It protects us from mass conformity, from being entangled in the 'lonely crowd' and saves us from being a product of what others expect of us. Seeing our calling in this light transforms our way of looking at the Christian life. Living the Christian life in a spirit of love transforms our approach of 'Do I really have to do this?' to one of 'How can I best respond to the unconditional and unlimited love of God?' It is the Spirit who inspires us to live in this way 'so that we might live no longer for ourselves but for Him' (Eucharistic Prayer IV).

Awareness of God's love for us brings with it a deep joy that comes as a precious gift of the Holy Spirit. It is a joy that not even suffering can disturb. It is a joy that shines from us unwittingly, without us even knowing it, making us people of Good News to a world that desperately needs it.

In the life, death and resurrection of Jesus Christ we see the personal and unconditional love of God revealed. Believing in that love gives birth to what we call faith. Faith is a response to the revealed love of God for us, his people. It is our 'yes' to the God who has loved us first.

Prayer:

> '*O God, you search me and you know me. You know my resting and my rising.*
> *Help me to see myself as you see me and to love myself as you love me.*
> *Make me more aware that I am precious and unique in your sight. Never allow me to turn aside to anything that offends the dignity that I enjoy by being your child. Give me security in my own identity as a person made in your image and likeness.*
> *May your love be the rock on which my life is built. Amen.*'

PART II

'I BELIEVE'

INTRODUCTION

As more and more people began to believe in the resurrection of Jesus, the Church began to grow and expand. The people who had come to experience God's love through Jesus Christ began to organise themselves and to prepare for the growth of Christianity. In order to do this effectively, especially for the benefit of new converts, they realised that what they believed needed to be expressed in writing, clearly and simply.

The Apostles' Creed was born in this way. It contains the essential beliefs of the Christian community. Every time we celebrate the Easter vigil, we renew the promises our parents made for us at baptism and that we ourselves made at our Confirmation. These are the public promises of faith we make in the articles contained in the Apostles' Creed. We reject Satan and choose God, accepting the gifts of life and love that Jesus came to give us:

> I believe in God the Father almighty,
> Creator of heaven and earth.
> I believe in Jesus Christ, his only Son, Our Lord.
> He was conceived by the power of the Holy Spirit and born of the Virgin Mary.
> He suffered under Pontius Pilate,
> Was crucified, died and was buried.
> He descended into hell.
> On the third day, he rose again.

He ascended into heaven, and is seated at the right hand of the Father.
He will come again to judge the living and the dead. I believe in the Holy Spirit,
The holy Catholic Church,
The communion of saints,
The forgiveness of sins,
The resurrection of the body,
And life everlasting. Amen.

Let us take a closer look at what is being said here in the Apostles' Creed. How can it speak to us in the context of our ordinary living? In order to answer this we will take the Creed one article at a time and try to unpack the good news that it contains.

Prayer:

'Lord, I believe in you, increase my faith. Fan into a flame that precious gift that you have given me so that I may know more of who you are and your goodness. Increase my appreciation of the gift of you calling me to be part of your family, the Church.
Every Sunday may I stand with my brothers and sisters and proclaim with new courage and conviction, my faith and trust in you. Amen.'

'I BELIEVE IN ONE GOD, THE FATHER ALMIGHTY, CREATOR OF HEAVEN AND EARTH'

The Wonder of Creation

At some point in history we are told that God's love was so strong that it could not contain itself and motivated by love, he took the initiative to bring creation into being so that creation could share his own life. God is love, God is the relationship of Father, Son and Spirit. It is the very nature of love to reach out, to share and to create different forms of life that are in relationship with one another. Every created thing resembles its author. From a painting we can tell something about the character of the artist. If this is true then it is a healthy spiritual exercise to take a fresh look with awe and wonder at the created world we are part of and learn more about its source and origin; namely the creative, loving power and presence we call God.

Admiring the beauty of creation raises our minds and hearts to him who was and is responsible for it all. It leads us to worship of him who is worthy of glory and honour. If created things resemble their author then creation gives us some clue as to how wonderful God must be. If creation is living, dynamic and colourful, then it points to a creator who is living, dynamic and loving. God is nothing like a watchmaker who makes his product, sets it in motion and then leaves it to its own devices. God is the one who creates, who recreates and whose spirit sustains creation in being.

Some of the spiritual giants of the Church had an awareness of this. St Francis of Assisi wrote at length about his closeness to God when he was close to nature. St Ignatius of Loyola would gaze into the night sky, caught up in prayer and contemplation as he pondered the majesty and immensity of God. For the saints, the heavens really did 'declare the glory of God' (Psalm 19:1). Many of our own parents and friends saw the gate of heaven everywhere with God smiling at them in every sunset and waving at them in every tree. Our Jewish ancestors also had a great appreciation for God the creator. For them, contemplation of God's creation was an essential part of prayer. They realised in prayer that the love of God that had been revealed to them was the same love that moved the planets, 'When I look at the heavens ... the moon and the stars ... what is man that you are mindful of him? Yet you have made him little less than a god and have crowned him with glory and honour' (Psalm 8:3-5). In glimpsing God's majesty, the psalmist understood both his own insignificance and his high calling. The insight did not crush him but moved him to praise God.

Later on we will reflect on the wonder and mystery of God becoming human. However, in order to appreciate this more we need to be aware of our absolute poverty and littleness in the presence of almighty God. This is not to put ourselves down in any way; it merely reminds us of our creatureliness, our limitations and our mortality. God did not have to create us, yet he did, out of love. He does not have to keep us in being, yet he does, out of love. It is his initiative. For this we praise him and offer thanks. We praise God for being God. This is pure worship. Impure worship seeks to extract favours from God or to force God's hand. It is like saying 'You owe me! I have honoured my part of the bargain now it is your turn'! We should always seek the God of consolation rather than the consolation of God. We seek the giver of the gifts and not the gifts of the giver.

Prayer:

'O God how great are your works! Open our eyes to see the beauty of creation that reflects your own goodness and love. Help us to recognise you in all you have made and may our hearts be moved to praise you O God of life, God of colour, God of the universe. Amen.'

The Human Person: Freedom to Love

Out of all the millions of species of living things that exist on planet earth, few can compare to the wonder and splendour of the human person. We are God's masterpiece. Our dignity lies in our faith that we are made in the image and likeness of God (cf. Genesis 1:26). What distinguishes the human person from any other life form on earth is our ability to enter into relationship with the God who created us, assisted by the unique gifts of intellect and will. Every human being is a reflection of the divine nature of God. From the very moment we were conceived in our mother's womb, we have a dignity and a worth that cannot be measured. Every person is a reflection of the love and the goodness of God.

However, questions remain. If humanity is so good then why do men and women inflict so much harm on one another? If God has made such a fine job of it, then why is the world full of suffering? If God is completely good and all powerful, then why is there evil in the world? Surely an all powerful God could do away with suffering if he wanted to?

However much parents love their children, they may still find themselves watching helplessly as their children make mistakes. They do not stop wanting the best for their children, but letting children grow up involves letting them make their own choices. Loving someone involves giving them the freedom to choose. No one can be forced to love. Love by its very nature has to be freely given and received. Even though God loves his creatures and wants them to be happy, he also wants them to love, and they can only do so if they are free. God has given us this freedom. We all have choices about how we want to live. We are free to choose whether or not to love. If God had 'rigged' his creation so that there was no possibility of us messing up, then our choices would not have been real choices and our love would have been a sham.

God is not responsible for the evil we do when we sin (we know that much of human suffering is caused directly or indirectly by humans themselves), but he does permit it. He permits it because he respects the freedom of the people he loves.

Prayer:

'O Lord, you search me and you know me,
you know if I am standing or sitting,
you read my thoughts from far away,
whether I walk or lie down, you are watching,
you know every detail of my conduct.

'You created my inmost self, knit me together in my
mother's womb.
For so many marvels, I thank you; a wonder am I and
all your works are wonders.

'You knew me through and through, my being held
no secrets from you,
When I was being formed in secret,
Textured in the depths of the earth.'[1]

---

1   Psalm 139.

The Trinity

The doctrine of the Trinity is a mystery. It is the mystery of God. Everything we can say about God seems to be matched by how much we don't know. God is eternal and is far beyond what our minds and hearts can understand.

The Trinity shows us that God is a God of relationship. The exchange of life and love that takes place among the Father, Son and Spirit is poured out on the world and freely offered to humanity.

It is in the very nature of God to reach out, to include, to share and to enter into relationship with his created world. We know from our own human nature that we are social beings, which should not surprise us when we come to realise that we are like the one who made us. We are made in his image and likeness.

Prayer:

> 'O Eternal Trinity, you are an abyss, a deep sea; you have given yourself to me – what greater could you give? You are a fire, ever burning and never consumed, consuming in your heat all the self-love of the soul, taking away all coldness. You are the garment that covers every nakedness. You feed the hungry in your sweetness, because you are gentle, without a trace of bitterness. O Eternal Trinity!'[2]

---

2   Catherine of Siena, 'The Dialogues of Catherine of Siena on Divine Revelation', *Catherine of Siena*, The Classics of Western Spirituality Series, New York: Paulist Press, 1990, Chapter 167.

The Circle of Life

As young children, a schoolyard game many of us were familiar with was 'ring-a-ring-a-rosy'. In the game a circle was formed where everyone held hands with their neighbour as they danced around in a circular motion. If you were looking on, it felt good to be noticed by someone and to see one of your friends break the chain of the circle and welcome you into it. You felt included and part of the life and fun of the group.

Theologians describe the inner life of the Trinity with a Greek word meaning 'to dance around'. This word conveys something of what the inner life of God is like, something like three people in a circle dancing around in the schoolyard or at a wedding. In the desire of God to share and to include, God has broken the circle in order to reach out to you and me so that we can share the life of the group, the very life of God. The Holy Spirit who 'blows where it wills' (John 3:8) is the one who reaches out to us and who enables us to experience the presence of God. From there the Spirit introduces us to Jesus the Son who invites us into a relationship with him, just like he did in the Gospels '... come and follow me' (Matthew 4:19). So too does the Spirit of Jesus bind us in relationship with our brothers and sisters around us. Once our relationship with the Lord Jesus is established, it is he who leads us to the Father our creator who has many rooms in his house, one of which has our name written on it with the words 'WELCOME'.

It is refreshing to think of God in this way. Many times we do not. For many of us God is still a harsh, dull, unchanging and grey character that we must please lest we experience the brunt of his anger. Rather, God as Trinity embraces us. The Church celebrates the Feast of the Most Holy Trinity every year on the first Sunday after Pentecost. However, we remember that every day is a feast of the Most Holy Trinity because God is always Trinity, always was and always will be.

Every time we bless ourselves, every time we pray, every time we worship, we do so in the name of God who is Father, Son and Spirit. We were baptised into the family life of God which is reflected and shared in the life of the Church. In that circle of life we find ourselves next to others who have also clasped the hand of welcome that God has extended, to become part of a new family and a new way of living. In that new life where we direct our worship to God and our service to each other, we experience growth, new life, friendship, understanding, forgiveness, acceptance, food, a purpose in life, discovery of who we are, inner peace ... In short the fullness of life that Jesus came to give us (cf. John 10:10).

Prayer:

'O Most Holy Trinity! Thank you for including me in your great circle of life. Thank you for welcoming me into your family. May I welcome others into my company as you have welcomed me into yours. Amen.'

Original Sin

'Tainted by Original Sin' – what does this mean? Traditionally we tried to understand original sin using images such as a 'stain' on our soul that baptism 'washed away'. This explained the urgency in years gone by to baptise children in case they died with this sin on their souls and risked being deprived of heaven. We also used to think of it in terms of the first sin that Adam committed, the consequences of which are still with us.

Our understanding has changed since then. We now understand 'original sin' not only as the historical sin of Adam but as a state in which all of us share. It is part of our human experience and something that we struggle with daily. It means that left to ourselves, we have a weakness in our human nature that leads to sin and a drifting away from God. It is the inclination we all experience towards our own selfishness. 'My will be done' is a desire that we all share but that is the direct opposite to another powerful desire that is addressed to God, 'Your will be done ...'. This is how we find ourselves and even when we want to do good we sometimes find ourselves doing the opposite. St Paul describes the dilemma brilliantly in a way that we can identify:

> I do not understand my own behaviour; I do not
> act as I mean to, but I do things I hate ... the good
> thing I want to do I never do; the evil thing which
> I do not want – this is what I do. In my inmost self
> I dearly love God's law, but I see that acting in my
> body there is a different law which battles against
> the law in my mind.[3]

It is this 'different law' that has come from original sin. This is what is meant when we describe ourselves as being part of 'fallen nature'. God gives us a special gift and ability at our baptism to rise above our human weaknesses, to choose good and to choose him.

Not that it happens without us or happens easily. It takes co-operation on our part with the promptings of the Holy Spirit and a spirit of prayerful dependency on God to come to the help of our weaknesses. It is the Holy Spirit who leads us to choose 'Thy will be done', for we believe that it is God alone who knows what is best for us. In his will is our peace.

---

3   Romans 7:15ff.

We don't always get it right. All of us know what it is like to struggle with our 'ego' or the part of us that instinctively seeks to satisfy our own needs first. In some sense, original sin can be described as an ongoing drama in our lives where we strive with God's grace to discover our true selves and to distance ourselves from our false selves and all forms of idolatry. This is the struggle that St Paul describes in his letter to the Romans. His true self or 'inmost self' is that which 'loves God's law'. His false self is that which 'battles against this law in my mind'. Nevertheless, we bear in mind that sinfulness or separation from God was never part of God's plan for humanity. These days it is common to hear the catchphrase '… but sure we are only human' when there is a human failing or as we try to come to terms with our weaknesses. Such a comment contains the truth that yes, we are a fallen nature and we all sin, but it is important to remind ourselves that sin is not part of being human. In fact the opposite is true. Sin distorts our humanity for God never wants humanity to be apart from him but rather to enjoy being in close relationship with him always.

Prayer:

'Come Holy Spirit to the help of my weaknesses.
Let them be not enemies but friends. Let them be the
cracks through which the light of your grace and love
shine, lighting up my life.
May my weaknesses lead me to you, to your support
and forgiveness.
For I know that with you, when I am weak, then I am
really strong. Amen.'

'And in Jesus Christ his Only Son Our Lord'

The Impact of his Life

Out of the billions of people who have inhabited the earth since the human family came into existence, no one has had as much influence as Jesus of Nazareth. The influence of his life was such that it prompted authorities to redefine the measurement of the passage of time based on his birth, which scholars say took place sometime between 4 and 6 BC. From then on, all the other events of history would be measured in relation to how long before or how long after they occurred since Jesus' birth.

The impact of Jesus' life is all the more remarkable for he lived in a primitive and pre-scientific age. Communication of his message lay at the heart of his mission and yet he did not enjoy the tools that we have at our disposal today. There were no microphones, no telephone, no e-mail, no internet, no cars, no trains, no planes. Here was a man who was a wandering preacher on foot who relied solely on his skills as a verbal communicator and the witness of his life. Despite what we would consider to be these huge obstacles to the effective communication of any message, the stories he told and the story of his life continue to capture the imagination of millions of people over two thousand years after his birth. The values he lived and the mission he began continue to inspire countless people to shape their attitudes and world view that they carry into daily life.

'Jesus is Lord' is a statement of faith in Christ's divinity that stands as the foundation stone of every Christian Church. It is a statement of faith that Jesus of Nazareth who lived and died, was raised from the dead by the Father's love and is still intimately present to his people all over the world.

The life of Jesus is as though we were turning a gem around so that it diffracts different rays of light. This allows us to appreciate its fuller beauty. Over two thousand years after his birth, the gem is still visible and is still being turned. Each turn reveals something new that speaks something more of the power of God's love that 'did not spare his only Son but gave him up for us all' (John 3:16).

Prayer:

'Christ be with me, Christ be before me, Christ be behind me,
Christ be in me, Christ be beneath me, Christ be above me, Christ be on my right, Christ be on my left,
Christ when I lie down, Christ when I sit down, Christ when I arise,
Christ be in every heart of everyone who thinks of me,
Christ be in the mouth of everyone who speaks of me,
Christ be in the eye of everyone that sees me,
Christ be in every ear that hears me.[1]

Fully Human and yet Divine

One of the things we may have assumed was that both Jesus himself and the people around him, including his mother and his disciples, knew from the very beginning that he was the Son

---

1   St Patrick's Breastplate.

of God. We may think of Jesus as all knowing, all seeing and therefore far removed from the rest of us who struggle to see, to know and to understand. We bear in mind that the Gospel accounts were written sixty years or more after the resurrection. A very important part of how all believers understand Jesus was clarified at one of the Church Councils way back in the fourth century. At that Council it was made clear that Jesus was both fully human and fully divine and that his two natures were not in competition with one another. Let us use our imagination for a moment and consider what those early years were like for Jesus of Nazareth.

When Jesus lay in the crib after his birth, he was the same as any newborn baby. He cried with the cold and with hunger. He found comfort and food at his mother's breast. As he grew up he had to learn the skills of carpentry in Joseph's workshop. In the synagogue he studied the faith of his ancestors and learned how to pray. He learned to love from the experience of being loved. He learned what it was to have a friend, to receive a gift, to be cheated and laughed at. He knew the feelings of self-worth, trust and obedience. He learned to watch and listen. He knew the joys of human love and its pains. He loved Judas, but Judas was to betray him. He grew in wisdom and knowledge like anybody else through his human experience, which shaped and formed his character. His divine nature did not allow him to have an advantage over others as if his learning was a matter of going through the motions or as if, as the Son of God, he knew it all already. At the heart of the Good News is the message that God comes to us through our common humanity that God himself took on in its fullness. It may be a little uncomfortable to think of Jesus as one who experienced tiredness, boredom, anger, frustration, sickness, disappointment, a shortage of money, sadness, attraction to women, darkness, being misunderstood, loneliness, fear, laughter, sorrow, joy and a host of other human emotions that are part of our lives. Yet if we believe that Jesus was fully human then these things were part of his life as they are part of ours. We recall what we pray at the Eucharist, 'He was human like us in all things but sin' (Eucharistic Prayer IV).

From the perspective of trying to understand Jesus' humanity, we can assume that when the people of Jesus' time looked at him, they did not say to themselves, 'There is God! Let us see how he acts'. Rather, those who lived with Jesus encountered an extraordinary and unique man but someone much like themselves, who shared with them the complexities and contradictions, the satisfactions and disappointments, the joys and sorrows of being human. They saw a man free enough to say what he believed and courageous enough to take the consequences; a man dedicated yet often frustrated; a man who sometimes went hungry and sometimes dined with the rich; a man who amazed the crowds but who couldn't retain the loyalty of one of his own; a man who had a special feeling for those who were hurt or lost, yet who was deserted by his own at the time of his greatest agony; a man whose whole disposition was towards mercy, forgiveness and non-violent resolution of conflict, yet who died by capital punishment.

What Jesus did through his divinity was to transform these human experiences in a way that gave them meaning and the hope that we might share in the blessings he won for us.

Prayer:

'Lord Jesus, through your spirit in my heart, you silently meet me in the events of my life. I cry out to you. The last strength of my heart reaches out for you. Let me find you, let me meet you in the whole of

my life so that slowly I also may come to understand what the Church tells me about you. As I put my hand into your wound, I say with the doubting and questioning Thomas: "My Lord and my God!"[2]

A Personal God Revealed

An experience common to most of us when we try to pray is that of being easily distracted. We come before God in prayer very often with thoughts of family, relationships, problems, worries, joys and a host of other things that make up daily life. It would be a mistake to think that our minds and hearts needed to be purified of all these things before we can come before God and have a real encounter with him. We must not think that our human experience must be cast aside if we are ready or worthy enough to meet God. We must never think of our humanity as an obstacle to our relationship with God or that our humanity in all its beauty and shadows is something to be ashamed of.

Jesus came with a message that was quite the contrary. He urged us to rejoice in our humanity as it is made in God's image and to thank God, as the Psalm says, 'for the wonder of my being'. Far from being distractions leading us away from God, the common human thoughts that arise for us in prayer may well be the means by which the Lord is drawing our attention to something that is very real and important in our lives. If something is important for us then it is important for God too. If something is bothering us then God is bothered too. He is never too big or busy to be unconcerned about anything that affects us. God provides for the birds of the air and yet Jesus tells

---

2   Karl Rahner, 'Meeting Jesus', *Prayers For a Lifetime*, New York: Crossroad, 1996, p. 82.

us 'Are you not worth much more than they are?' (Matthew 6:26).

With the life of Jesus Christ, God was revealed as a personal God who knows all his children by name. This is expressed by the powerful image of the Good Shepherd that Jesus called himself in the Gospel of St John: 'I am the Good Shepherd. I know my sheep and they know me' (John 10:14).

Just as a shepherd knows his sheep, Jesus reveals to us that God knows all of us personally, better than we know ourselves. Why? Because he made us, God our creator and re-creator is with us always and is continually reforming us, recreating us, maturing us, preparing us through the experiences of everyday life. This happens by the power of the Holy Spirit, received at Baptism, who dwells within us. How we are, how we are feeling, how we are coping is of the utmost importance to God as he showed us through the words and actions of Jesus. He is the Good Shepherd who has a special love for the lost sheep (cf. Matthew 15:24; Luke 15:4-7), for the person who has lost their way; for the sinner, for the struggler (cf. Luke 5:31ff). He is the personal God who loves us personally. Through the life of Jesus we see the care that God has for each one of us as his children whose names are inscribed on the palm of his hand.

When we ponder what the Gospels tell us about Jesus, we cannot help but be moved and reassured. In Luke chapter 15 (The Lost Sheep, The Lost Coin, The Prodigal Son) we see how enormously sensitive and caring he was to those who had lost their way. Anyone who feels depressed and who fears rejection by God should read quietly the whole of that chapter. Whatever may be the burden of sin or guilt we carry, God is always there waiting for us. He searches for us urgently but waits patiently. He does not force us.

Prayer:

'Father, we honour the heart of your Son
broken by man's cruelty,
yet symbol of love's triumph,
pledge of all that man is called to be.
Teach us to see Christ in the lives we touch,
To offer him living worship
By love filled service to our brothers and sisters.
We ask this through Christ Our Lord. Amen.'[3]

The Loving Parent

The revelation of God as a personal God was a major difficulty for the Jews. For them, God was very 'other' and holy. The thought of God becoming what he himself had made was simply absurd. So highly revered was God in the life of the Jews that the name of God could only be used sparingly because of the unworthiness of those who used it. For the Jews, the name of someone expressed who they were, so when Jesus began to address God with a new name, we can imagine that it caused quite a stir. The name he used for God was the Aramaic word 'Abba', which translates as 'daddy' or 'papa'. As the name suggests, Jesus related to the Father in a way that was personal, intimate and loving, similar to the way a child relates to a parent it trusts completely. This image of a child living under the loving gaze of its mother/father was not completely new to the Jewish mind. There are images in the Old Testament that compare the love of God for the Jewish people to that of a

---

3   Opening Prayer: *Mass of Sacred Heart of Jesus.*

mother and her child; 'Can a woman forget her baby at the
breast, feel no pity for the child she has borne? Even if these
were to forget, I shall never forget you' (Isaiah 49: 15). However,
while it was acceptable to think of the Jewish people as God's
beloved child, to refer to yourself as such was an entirely
different matter.

Jesus was acutely aware that God was his loving Father and
that he was God's loving Son. From the very beginning of his
ministry, it became clear that Jesus had a unique relationship
with his Father. The Gospel accounts of his baptism in the
Jordan convey how Jesus experienced himself as someone
special in God's eyes: 'This is my Son the Beloved; my favour
rests on him' (Matthew 3:17; Mark 1:11; Luke 3:22). The rest of
the Gospel demonstrates the practical effect of holding fast to
these words pronounced at the Lord's baptism. This intense,
deep and intimate relationship that Jesus had with his Father
was the rock of his life and coloured everything he thought,
said and did. Especially at the lowest moments, Jesus sought
strength in the source that had never failed him before and that
encouraged him forward. While in agony in the garden on the
night before he died he prayed that the chalice of suffering
might pass him by, but only if it was consistent with the Father's
will (cf. Luke 22:42). What gave him the strength to endure his
passion and cruel loneliness on the cross was the belief that
despite his life ending in humiliation, agony and apparent
failure, he had been faithful and loyal to his Father and that he
had done nothing wrong. Despite many temptations, he had
never hedged on a commitment to the Father and never
deviated from the rule of living by self-giving love. He trusted
in the word he heard from his Father and refused to give up his
freedom or to compromise the primacy of love as the rule of
his life. For Jesus, faithfulness to the Father came with a heavy
price. He died as he lived, trusting that life was not a bad joke

and that his questions about life would not echo into an empty future. He died as he lived believing in himself because he trusted that God believed in him. With no proof of the resurrection, Jesus died on the cross hoping against hope that the God in whom he trusted would have the final say. The voice of the Father at his baptism echoed in his ear, 'This is my Son, the Beloved; my favour rests on Him' (Matthew 3:17). That voice carried him through life and shielded him from the baggage of bitterness, jealousy or resentment.

There is something very natural and instinctive in us that looks to the guidance and love of a parent. Perhaps this is something of what St Paul had in mind in his letter to the Galatians when he spelt out Jesus' message of this new way of relating to God as a loving parent who is intimately close to us. It is the life-giving intimacy with God of which he wants us to partake. Jesus remained a child of his Father and said to his followers, 'Unless you become like little children, you will never enter the kingdom of heaven' (Matthew 18:3). The invitation of God to relate to him as a loving parent is a call to see ourselves as we really are.

The parent/child relationship that we enjoy with God is not one that maintains us in childish dependency. Instead his grace invites us towards maturity and ultimately towards freedom. But it is not a freedom that comes with being completely independent of others. God's gift of freedom can only be discovered in being interdependent with others and with God. No matter how independently we live our lives from each other and from God, no matter how unbelieving we claim to be, underneath all our accomplishments and successes there is an inner child within us that craves to be held safe and loved without condition. The psychologists tell us that the way children related to their parents has a huge bearing on how they relate to others later on in adulthood. The same is true of God.

Relating to God is like relating to a loving parent in a healthy and trusting way that affects all our relationships for the better. Relating to God is equivalent to allowing ourselves to be held in that loving embrace and saying 'yes' to his gift of unconditional love.

Prayer:

'Blessed be Jesus who is always near in times of stress. Even when we cannot feel his presence, he is close.
Jesus said within my heart, 'I will never leave you either in happiness or distress. I will always be there to help you and watch over you. Nothing in heaven or earth can part you from me.
When you are quiet and still, I can speak to your heart.'[4]

4   Margery Kempe. Taken from *The Mirror of Love: Daily Readings With Margery Kempe*, G. Hawker (ed.), London: Darton, Longmann & Todd, 1988.

'He was Conceived by the Power of the Holy Spirit and Born of the Virgin Mary'

Mary, Model of Faith

The life of Mary, the mother of Jesus, reminds us of the extravagance of the love of God who choose her and whose choice made her 'full of grace'. Mary's greatest gift lay in her selection by God to be the mother of his Son. God wanted his Son to be born of her but not before she had agreed to it. The angel Gabriel was sent by God to ask her for her trust and co-operation with his plan. At that moment, Mary represented the human race of all generations in accepting the gift of a Saviour. As St Bernard of Clairvaiux once wrote, the whole world fell silent as it awaited her response. Her *'fiat'* or 'yes' to God's plan for her life meant that humanity would never be the same again, restoring a future of hope for all time. It was the greatest turning point that history has ever known.

God's choice of Mary was not a reward for anything she did. Because God chose Mary to be mother of Jesus, all generations, including our own, call her blessed. Her mission in God's plan was to offer the life of her Son to every generation of the human family.

Many of us still think of Mary as one who had it easier than the rest of us and so as one who is difficult to accept as a model. This may be because we tend to see her almost as a goddess rather than as a human being like us.

Certainly Mary has a unique role. Being chosen did not exclude her from making a choice. Mary could have used her freedom to say 'yes' or 'no' to God's request of her. Indeed we would certainly have understood had she made another response to the angel Gabriel, asking for time to think about it or to ask more questions. After all, she was being asked to accept something that was going to change her life forever. Not only that, but the consequences of acceptance were frightening. She who was preparing for marriage would now find herself mysteriously pregnant which would bring her great shame, put her life in danger and risk destroying her relationship with Joseph her future husband. In short, she was being asked to let go of everything in order to trust. However, the assurances that God made through Gabriel were enough for her. He would not let her down or deceive her.

The difference between Mary and ourselves is not that Mary was chosen and we are not. We too are chosen. The difference lies in her response. Hers was total and was based on her unconditional trust in God's love for her. We would like to think that ours is total but most of the time it is not. We can be half-hearted and sometimes our response is more to our own will than it is to God's. Despite this, God never gives up on us and always invites us to respond in faith to his call. As St Paul reminds us, 'He chose us, he chose us in Christ, to be holy and spotless and to live through love in his presence' (Ephesians 1:4). Like Mary, we face God's choice of us, for we too are highly favoured by him. Like her we are invited to say 'yes' to God and to trust. Like Mary we may be asked to let go of much and to make a great act of faith. With Mary we pray that we may have the same faith in God's word and goodness so that we may make her response our own, 'I am the handmaid of the Lord, let what you have said be done to me' (Luke 1:38).

Prayer:

'Mary, Our Mother, help us to believe that God has
also chosen us for a special task or vocation in life.
By your prayers, help us to rejoice that we too are
highly favoured by God. Teach us to know God's will
for our lives and to do it with love. Make our "yes"
like yours with deep trust in God's plans that we
know are perfect. Throughout our lives, may we join
with you in praising God forever as we say, "For the
Almighty has done great things for me, holy is his
name". Amen.'

The Immaculate Conception

The dogma of the Immaculate Conception is celebrated by the
Western Church each year on 8 December and by the Eastern
Church on the following day. The doctrine of the Immaculate
Conception was announced by Pope Pius IX in 1854 but was
widely believed in the Church long before that. It states that
'from the first moment of her conception by a singular grace
and privilege of Almighty God and by virtue of the merits of
Jesus Christ, Mary was preserved immune from all stain of
original sin' (*Ineffabilis Deus*, 1854). But what does all this mean?
Firstly, Mary was enriched by God with gifts appropriate to her
unique role as mother of Christ. Because she was to be mother
to the Son of God and for him to take his human nature from
her, it was fitting that at all times, even from her conception,
she would be in perfect relationship with God. It was
inconceivable that sin, or separation from God, would be part
of her life at any stage because of her relationship to her Son.
This is why the Church has referred to her down the ages as
'full of grace'. As the wording of the dogma suggests, Mary

was preserved from the state of original sin by the grace of God and by the saving work of her Son. In this sense, Mary is redeemed and transformed like the rest of humanity.

Secondly, the dogma concerns all of us as Church. Mary, as the first Christian, accepted the word of God so completely that literally, the Word of God, Jesus Christ was born of her. As such, she represents the Church before God. With the Church she contemplates God's word and his saving love for his people. What happened to her we hope will happen to us. The dogma of the Immaculate Conception shows us the beauty of a person in perfect relationship with God as Father, Son and Holy Spirit. The life of every Christian is called to show forth Jesus Christ perfectly. Together in community we strive to be 'true images' of Jesus, full of grace like Mary.

As Christians who are on a journey of growth through life and who strive to become more Christ like, Mary is the perfect example of one who, by God's grace, has reached that final goal for which we aim. In our struggle, Mary is our mother, our friend and our companion on the journey.

Prayer:

'*Father, the image of the Virgin is found in the Church. Mary had a faith that your Spirit prepared and a love that never knew sin for you kept her sinless from the first moment of her conception.*
Trace in our actions the lines of her love, in our hearts her readiness of faith. Prepare once again a world for your Son who lives and reigns with you and the Holy Spirit, one God forever and ever. Amen.'[1]

---

1 Opening Prayer: *Mass of Immaculate Conception.*

*'O Mary conceived without sin, pray for us who have
recourse to thee.'*[2]

The Assumption

Scientists tells us that every one of the stars is a sun and some
suns are so big that they could contain the sun that we see, the
earth and the distance between them. At a conservative
estimate there are 100 million galaxies! Science also tells us
that, amazingly, to our knowledge, planet earth is the only
place in the universe where life exists. Furthermore, out of all
the millions of species of life that exist on the earth, the
human race enjoys a special dignity. For us as believers, this is
because the Creator of the universe freely chose, out of love,
to become one of us. Looking on the incarnation in this light
brings us to a new and deeper awareness of our dignity and
our calling. It 'assumes' us to a new level of dignity, of
knowing who we are, where we have come from and where we
are going.

The doctrine of the Assumption of Mary was defined by
Pope Pius XII in 1950. Like the Immaculate Conception, the
dogma of faith was believed in long before it was made official
by the Church. It came at a time of strong devotion to Mary in
the Church as a whole, four years before the Marian year of
1954. It also came shortly after the end of the Second World
War where there had been such wastage of human life. The
dogma of the assumption put before the Church and the world
once again the dignity of every human person as made in the
image and likeness of God. It also spoke afresh about the
destiny to which humanity is called.

---

2   Prayer of the Miraculous Medal.

Similar to the Immaculate Conception, the assumption is not about the glorification of Mary alone but of the whole people of God. It speaks to us of our role in the ongoing drama of how God saves his people and the change which Jesus Christ effects for the human race.

The words 'assumed into heaven' can conjure up misleading images as to what happened Mary after she died. The heaven to which Mary was assumed was not a region in the skies but rather a new level of existence before God. Therefore we can say that Mary's assumption is about a transformation of the human condition from its familiar earthly state to a new way of being in which it shares fully the life and glory of God. The closeness of Jesus and Mary is being asserted here for their companionship on earth could not be broken, even by death. Mary's assumption is the fulfilment of the Lord's promise not only to Mary but to all of us that 'Where I am, there you will be also' (John 14:3).

Just as Mary is inseparable from the Lord, so is his Church. The assumption is a sign of the Lord's promise that he would glorify his disciples and lead us to the destiny to which he called us: 'The glory that you have given me, I have given them' (John 17:22). In Mary we see one who has already reached that goal where we hope to follow. The dogma of the Assumption is one of the most hopeful and encouraging articles of the Church's belief. It has many implications. It reminds us that we are God's Church and that we cannot utterly depart from him unless we really want to. It is a glimpse of the final glory that is ours as promised by Christ. It is not to be understood as a once off historical event but as a continuous process that is going on at this very moment. Whenever in the Church here on earth there is a prayer offered, an act of charity, a hand extended, there is assumption, there is human life being lifted up by God to God.

Prayer:

'Almighty Father of Our Lord Jesus Christ, you have revealed the beauty of your power by exalting the lowly virgin of Nazareth and making her the mother of Our Saviour. May the prayers of this woman clothed with the sun bring Jesus to the waiting world and fill the void of incompletion with the presence of her child who lives and reigns with you and the Holy Spirit, one God forever and ever. Amen.'[3]

Mary for the Future

The challenge for us as Christians today is to regain a true and living awareness of Mary's presence with us in the Church in order that we may understand our Christian faith more fully. It means reclaiming Mary as one of us, as human, and as one who stands with us in relating to God. In the past perhaps we tended to associate many of the feminine qualities of God with Mary before we realised that God was both male and female. This among other reasons tended to attribute divine qualities to Mary that rightly belonged to God. If and when this happens, a great disservice is done to God and to Mary by seeing her as a kind of 'back door' in securing favours from God that he may not otherwise grant.

Mary is the model of Christian discipleship who teaches us that our 'yes' to God is to be total and from the depths of our being. She reminds us that 'all things will work to the good for those who love God' (cf. Romans 8:28). She teaches us that God is a God who is on our side, the one who waits on us at

---

3   Opening Prayer: *Mass of the Assumption.*

table and who washes our feet. She teaches us how to see the goodness of God in everything and everyone and how to rejoice in it. Adopting her attitude we find ourselves with thankful hearts filled with gratitude for the saving things that God has done in our lives. With her our hearts can pray in gratitude, 'For the Almighty has done great things for me, holy is his name' (Luke 1:47). This is something invaluable in a consumer world that seeks to achieve more and more without taking the time to give thanks. She is the one who points to her Son as a person in whom the world can find happiness and peace. With tender love, she never ceases to point to her Son and say to us, 'Do whatever he tells you' (John 2:5).

The Immaculate Conception and Assumption are lights of hope when we look at the events of history with our enormous record of pain and suffering. Without God, humanity can very easily degenerate towards fatalism, destruction and despair. We saw this in the last century with Nazism and Communism, two regimes that excluded God. Both systems collapsed eventually but not before they left a trail of blood and destruction behind them. Have we learned the lessons of history? Do we still believe the words of the serpent in the Garden of Eden who tempted Adam and Eve to do the very same and to live without God? As one of us, Mary pleads with humanity not to make the same mistakes over and over again. She is a sign of someone who lived a full life of love and freedom which was made possible by her being always in relationship with God. True devotion to her always leads us back to the truth about ourselves, about Christ and about the world.

Mary helps us in her witness to true fulfilment and how it can be attained. Without her example and inspiration we could be tempted to believe that true happiness is an achievement and not a gift. This is not the wisdom of Christianity. The whole life of Jesus was one of self-emptying, self-giving. Self-fulfilment for the Christian comes in self-emptying. We must die to ourselves.

Mary, surely, is a perfect model of this process of active self-emptying. She lived for others and for the mission of her Son, with which she is so closely identified. She was prepared to put her own ambitions and plans for her life aside for the love of her God and what he was asking of her. She realised that God had been generous to her and so she was generous to him. She knew that she received without charge. She is a model of someone who responded by giving without charge. She gave her word and her life to God. In response, God was lavish with his gifts. Mary stands out as an example of someone who gave for the kingdom of God and who was repaid a hundredfold in return, as Jesus promised (cf. Matthew 10:42).

We must be careful when we interpret those beautiful words of Mary in Luke where she responds to the angel, 'I am the handmaid of the Lord, let what you have said be done to me' (1:37). Her desire to do God's will does not mean that she was passive, submissive and meek. She was a woman of unbelievable strength who experienced poverty, the lot of a refugee and the unspeakable sight of watching her Son die on a cross. The disciples fled but she did not flee. She stayed with a mother's courage, a mother's fidelity, a mother's goodness and a faith that did not waver in the hour of darkness. Having endured all of this she is still found with the other disciples praying in the upper room with her faith intact, waiting for God to fulfil what he promised (cf. Acts 1:12-14). Because this is true and because she remained steadfast in the face of trial, she remains close to all in any kind of difficulty.

Mary is also a model and example for our world today in her fidelity, not only to God's word but to her own. Her 'yes' to God's will that she uttered with her lips was matched by her 'yes' that she lived with her life. Her 'yes' meant 'yes'. She gave her word and by God's grace, she kept it. As such, Mary's life was like a transparent pane of glass. What we see is what we get. Because she was and remains a person who is deeply authentic and sincere, she is a shining alternative for modern times to any kind of superficiality. She was a human being with depth and integrity who was impregnated with God's life. The seed that was God's word did not meet a shallow soil in her heart. The seed was received by a fertile and rich soil that produced fruit 'a hundredfold' (cf. Luke 8:8). She is a model to all of us of a life of commitment. She was faithful to the end, being there at the beginning of Christ's life, there with him throughout it, there at the end of it and there at Pentecost in the days of the early Church. She has always been with the disciples of her Son because she is one of them. She is with us still.

In recent times we as Church are becoming increasingly aware of our responsibility to be people of justice and to challenge injustice and hypocrisy wherever we find it. In today's divided world, Mary stands in solidarity with those who are oppressed and dominated or treated unjustly in any way. She is a prophet who announces that God will reverse the order of things when 'He pulls down princes from their thrones and raises high the lowly' (Luke 1:52). She is a symbol of hope and an icon of a new humanity set free; a humanity consisting of equals where there are no injustices based on power and self-seeking. Mary, conceived without sin, is one of our own who reminds us of our calling to become part of and shape a new world of peace and justice where Christ is all in all. May Mary always be our friend and guide who leads us to God.

Prayer:

'Mary our Mother, you have always had a special
place in the hearts of the Irish people.
Continue to pray for us your children and intercede
for us before God.
Help us to be like you so that every aspect of our lives
may be a total "yes" to what God wants.
To you we entrust our future. To you we entrust our
children and families. Teach us how to follow your
Son and to appreciate how much God loves us.
Amen.'

'HE BECAME MAN'

Introduction

The central mystery of Christianity, underlining everything else, is the mystery of the incarnation. God in his wisdom became a human being. It is worth pausing for a while to reflect on the fact that Jesus took on our humanity. Do we think of him as coming down from heaven, remaining on earth for thirty-three years and then going back home? Do we think of Jesus as having been on earth for this short time but who now has returned to heaven where he stays and looks upon us at a distance? Was the incarnation a thirty-year year experiment, a once-off incursion by God into human history? This way of thinking uses the past tense for the incarnation. This is misleading because the Church believes that the incarnation is still an ongoing mystery being as real and present in the world today as it was in Jesus' time. Let us consider the mystery of the incarnation under three headings: (i) the 'Why' of the incarnation; (ii) the physical character of the incarnation; and (iii) its ongoing character.

Prayer:

'Father, today you fill our hearts with joy as we recognise in Christ the revelation of your love.
No eye can see his glory as our God,
Yet now he is seen as one like us.

*Christ is your Son before all ages, yet now he is born
in time.*
*He has come to lift all things to himself, to restore
unity to creation and to lead humankind from exile
into your heavenly kingdom.*
*With all the angels of heaven we sing our joyful
hymn of praise.*"

'He Became Human' – Why?

Why did God become one of us? Jesus of Nazareth could be
seen, heard and touched by those who knew him. He was a
real, historical figure and through him, God became physically
present in the world. As one generation of Christians told
another about Jesus, they were anxious to emphasise that their
experience of this person was one that was concrete and real.
As St John teaches us, the mystery of Christ was 'Something
which existed since the beginning, which we have heard, which
we have seen with our own eyes, which we have watched and
touched with our hands: The Word of life: this is our theme' (1
John 1:1).

Through Jesus, God spoke to us in the language of our
common humanity in ways we could all understand. Jesus
Christ became the language of God in human form. Jesus is the
Word of God who came to reveal who God really is. Though
fully human, the fullness of God dwelt within him. As the eyes
of a human cannot look directly at the sun without being
blinded, neither can we look directly at God. The following
verse of a Christmas poem puts it well, 'Man cannot see God
and live, the sight of my glory would be too much, so I turned

---

1   Preface: Mass for Christmas.
2   B. Swan, *Through the Eyes of the Father at Christmas*, Unpublished.

its volume down in Christ, for him to see, to hear and touch'.[2]

With the incarnation, God has turned down his splendour so that we can see, hear, touch, smell and taste his presence. As we pray at Mass during Christmas, 'In him we see our God made visible and so are caught up in the love of the God we cannot see' (Preface of Christmas). As St Paul reminds us, God has poured his divinity onto the world with Jesus who 'emptied himself' in loving service, offering to all a share in the same divinity that the Father had lavished on him (cf. Philippians 2:7). Even today, the fragrance of this love poured out fills the whole world.

Prayer:

'Father all powerful and ever living God, we do well always and everywhere to give you thanks through Jesus Christ Our Lord.
Today in him, a new light has dawned upon the world: God has become one with humanity and humanity has become one again with God.
Your eternal Word has taken upon himself our human weakness,
Giving our mortal nature immortal value.
So marvellous is this oneness between God and humanity that in Christ man restores to man the gift of everlasting life.
In our joy we sing to your glory with all the choirs of angels.'[3]

---

3 Preface: Mass for Christmas.

Touched by God

The English word 'incarnation' comes from the Latin word 'carnus' meaning flesh. The word 'in-carnation' means 'in the flesh', or something that is visible, physical and tangible. Jesus was not a symbolic presence or a representative presence but *the* actual presence of God in the world he himself had made. The healing, forgiveness and love that Jesus offered were not abstract concepts or words from a distance, but were real gifts that came through real contact with people. The Gospels are littered with examples of Christ's love in action.

He put his fingers into the deaf man's ears and touched his tongue with spittle (cf. Mark 7:33). He put spittle on the eyes of the blind man who was healed (cf. Mark 8:23). Jesus loved the company of children and to show his affection for them 'he laid his hands on them, embraced them and gave them his blessing' (cf. Mark 10:16). We are told also by Mark that he raised the daughter of Jairus from the dead by 'taking the child by the hand' (5:41) and of people being brought to him whom they 'begged him to touch' (cf. Mark 8:22). He even touched and healed a man who 'had a virulent skin disease' (cf. Matthew 8:3; Mark 1:40; Luke 5:13), something that would have excluded Jesus from public worship in the eyes of the Jews. The Jews were scandalised when Jesus allowed people to touch him, especially those who were considered unclean and outcasts by the Pharisees. The woman who was a sinner wept at his feet and wiped them with her hair, prompting the Pharisees to say, 'If this man were a prophet, he would know who this woman is who is touching him and what a bad name she has' (Luke 7:39). Another beautiful episode from the Gospel is where Jesus cured the woman with the haemorrhage. Jesus asked who had 'touched' him for 'I felt that power had gone out of me' (Luke 8:46).

Jesus made real contact with people. His love was mediated through concrete signs and in ways that people could experience. It was a love 'in-carnate' or 'in-the-flesh'. So too did people make real contact with Jesus by coming to him and 'touching him', allowing the life and power of God to gush into their lives.

When we consider the mystery of the incarnation today, we struggle to appreciate that God's love comes to us in the same hands-on way as it does in the Scriptures. Maybe we find it difficult because we tend to imagine that the Jesus who touched people with love in the Gospels and the Jesus to whom we now pray and relate, are not quite the same. Perhaps we think that the saving work of Jesus we see in the Gospels as tangible and visible all came to an end with his ascension into heaven, from where he still loves and saves his people but in a less real or somewhat removed way. The problem seems to be in our belief that the Church as the 'Body of Christ' still mediates the saving 'touch' and 'embrace' of Jesus in a way that brings his love close and continues to show his care for the world in definite and concrete ways. But God never loves us less, only more. Having drawn so close to us in his earthly life, he did not withdraw into the distance. At Bethlehem, we glimpsed his 'touch', his 'embrace', his nearness. Through Mary, God's love became visible and was born. That is our gift and calling too.

Prayer:

'Father, thank you for sending us Jesus your Son to reveal how much you love us. Draw us deeper into the mystery of how closely you have united yourself to us in body and soul. Bless our parish community. May others recognise in our way of living your presence in the world and that truly, God continues to live among us with whom he is well pleased.

*We ask this through Our Lord Jesus Christ who lives
and reigns with you and the Holy Spirit, One God
forever and ever. Amen.'*

Giving Birth to God

If we are the Body of Christ, filled with the Spirit of Christ then
it means that the mystery of the incarnation that began with
Jesus continues up to this very moment. We must think of it in
the present tense and not only in the past. Even though the
earthly life of Jesus was a unique time in history, it does not
mean that we who never knew the earthly Jesus, are loved less
by God or have less advantage than those who encountered
him in first century Palestine. As part of the community of
believers or the family of the Church, we have access to the
same saving presence of Christ. United in the Holy Spirit, we
are 'One body, one Spirit in Christ' (Eucharistic Prayer III). It
means that through us as believers, God can still be heard, seen
and touched. We are God's physical hands, his feet, his mouth
and his heart in the world. The Christian God therefore,
continues to live among his people in a real and historical way.
He is present and active in time, space and history.

The implications of this awesome mystery, colour every
aspect of how we relate to God and to each other: how we pray,
how we look for healing and reconciliation, how we seek
guidance and how we understand community, religious
experience and mission. It makes us realise that God continues
to work through his people because he has united himself
irreversibly to us. It means that we as a community are called to
mediate God's 'touch' and blessing to the world as Jesus did. It
makes us more aware of how much God is dependent on us to
continue the work he began with Jesus his Son. It calls us to
social action and responsibility. It challenges us to be less passive

to injustices going on around us and reminds us of our calling to create a civilisation of love in God's name. Because of the incarnation, every encounter we have with another human being is never just another meeting. Every encounter is a unique moment when we can touch another person's life with the presence of God. When God is present or 'incarnate', the effects of his 'touch' are the same as they were in the Gospels: healing, forgiveness, reconciliation, justice and new life.

The incarnation was not a thirty-three year experiment by God in history. God did not draw very close to us with Jesus and then move away. Through us, the mystery of the incarnation still goes on.

Prayer:

'Father, thank you for creating me. Thank you for giving my life meaning.
You have called me to be part of building your kingdom on earth as it is in heaven. Help me to live my Christian calling with faithfulness to your Word and example. Support me with the encouragement and inspiration of my fellow Christians.
I ask this through Christ Our Lord who lives and reigns with you and the Holy Spirit, one God forever and ever. Amen.'

'I BELIEVE IN ONE LORD JESUS CHRIST WHO SUFFERED UNDER PONTIUS PILATE, WAS CRUCIFIED, DIED AND WAS BURIED'

Introduction

Jesus was born in Bethlehem about 4 BC and was raised in Nazareth. During that time, history and the Gospels record that Israel was occupied by the Romans. The Romans were hated by the Jews as foreign invaders of their country and were the subject of many revolts and uprisings. To counteract these threats, the Romans developed a well-earned reputation as brutal rulers who made terrible examples of those who threatened them. Crucifixion was a particularly cruel form of capital punishment that entailed a slow and agonising death. Not only this but the helpless victim was subject to many other humiliating cruelties before and during their agony. Every shred of human dignity was stripped away. Thus crucifixion as a means of execution did not stop with physical torture, but struck at the very soul of the victim, attempting to desecrate him.

When we come to approach the suffering and death of the Lord we walk on holy ground. All attempts to understand the workings of God inevitably fail because we are dealing with a profound mystery. This fact, however, should not put us off contemplating the death of our Saviour. We consider his death from three perspectives: (i) the context of his death; (ii) Jesus' death and God's will; and (iii) tthe mystery of suffering and death.

Prayer:

'Almighty and ever living God, you have given the human race Jesus Christ Our Saviour as a model of humility.
He fulfilled your will by becoming man and giving his life on the cross.
Help us to bear witness to you by following his example of suffering and make us worthy to share in his resurrection.
Grant this through Christ Our Lord. Amen.' [1]

The Lord's Death

From the very beginning of his life, Jesus stood as a witness to the truth and was not afraid to bring it to bear despite how unpopular it might be. As he approached Jerusalem, he knew that if he continued to preach his message there at the heart of Jewish worship and Roman rule, his life would be in grave danger. From a human perspective, it was a prospect over which he must surely have worried and felt fear. Nevertheless there could be only one outcome. The work of his Father came first. He must be faithful to the work the Father had given him to do. He had to bear witness to the truth. Before Pilate he sums up the reason for his entire mission: 'I was born for this, I came into the world for this, to bear witness to the truth' (John 18:37). The story of what happened next is familiar to us. He was welcomed initially by the people as he rode into the city on a donkey, symbolic of one who comes in peace. The Jewish

---

1   Opening Prayer: Mass on Passion Sunday.

leaders conspired with one of his close followers to hand him over to the Jewish court, the Sanhedrin. There he was accused, by lying witnesses, of blasphemy and other false charges. He was then handed over to the Romans as a blacklisted troublemaker and portrayed as a threat to the Roman establishment.

In the end it was left to Pilate to pronounce sentence. Before he did so he consulted the mood of the fickle crowd who shouted for his death – the same crowd who welcomed Jesus into their city only a week before. 'Pilate then gave his verdict: their demand was to be granted. He released the man they asked for who had been imprisoned because of rioting and murder, and handed Jesus over to them to deal with as they pleased' (Luke 23:24).

Prayer:

'Lord Jesus, from the beginning to the end of your life on earth, your food was to do the will of the One who sent you. Even in the face of death, you were faithful to your Father. May we never accept anything that is contrary to your will for our lives. Inspire us to bear witness always to the truth and to remain true to ourselves. Amen.'

Suffering and Death: God's Will?

When we come to appreciate the context in which Jesus died, it seems inaccurate to describe Jesus' death simply as 'God's will'. It seems more accurate to describe his death as the result of evil collusion between the Jewish leaders and the Romans. Another way of looking on it is to say that Jesus' death resulted from him doing as he always had done, that is bearing witness to the truth.

Someone had to confront the darkness and sin that had arisen in human hearts that threatened to destroy us. We needed a Saviour. Jesus is seen in the New Testament as confronting things like sickness, death and the pain of isolation. He was a victim of sinners' violence, taking every kind of filth and cruelty on to himself, so much so that 'The crowds were appalled on seeing him, so disfigured did he look that he seemed no longer human' (Isaiah 52:14; 53:6). Jesus allowed himself to be this victim, taking the sin of the world onto himself: 'He was pierced through for our faults, crushed for our sins' (Isaiah 53:5). In allowing his only Son to undergo this agony, God thought only of us. Only the greatest love ever known could allow this tragedy to happen, the love of God for his people. This was the price that God was willing to pay so that we might be saved and united in that same love. Because of what Jesus did for us, because he willingly took responsibility for our sin, 'On him lies a punishment that brings us peace and through his wounds we are healed' (Isaiah 53:5). As his death approached Jesus realised the price to be paid in coming so close to the powers of evil and setting his people free. Yet such was the depth of his love that it was a price he was willing to pay. Despite the natural fear of dying that he experienced Jesus knew that this was what he must do. This for him was God's will. It had to come first and it did: 'My food is to do the will of him who sent me and to accomplish his work' (John 4:34).

Even during his trial and execution he was surrounded by people he loved. He loved Judas who had betrayed him; he loved Peter who had denied him; he loved those who scourged him and who nailed him to the cross. He went to his death reaching out his hand in saving love to those who handed him over, his executioners and even those who died with him. Jesus died in total solidarity with sinners, the broken of mind and body, with all victims of violence. Jesus' death for the sake of all was a triumph of the Father's love and his own, a love that even death could not destroy. In his crushed and battered body he represented the world's 'no' to God, to grace and to salvation. Yet by his obedience to the Father's will he was at the same time God's 'yes' to the world.

Since the beginning of time, humanity has struggled with reconciling the problem of evil with the concept of an all loving and all powerful God. The question of God allowing terrible calamities and atrocities to take place will not go away. We ask why does he not act? But what kind of action do we want? Do we want a god who sees what is wrong with the world and then comes with the weapons and means to put things right? Surely this god would destroy the oppressors and evil people in the world, feed the hungry, cure all illnesses and 'fix' everything that needs fixing?

The God of Jesus Christ does not respond to violence with more violence. The only violence he knows and shows is the violence of unconditional love for his created world. Even if the response of someone is to spit back in his face, God's response is to love even more. Such was the way of Jesus throughout his passion and such is the way of God. In this sense, Jesus personifies perfectly the love St Paul described as not 'insisting on its own way' (1 Corinthians 13:5). It may grieve God that his love is rejected but he can do no other than love, for love is his nature; 'God is love' (1 John 4:8). The life and death of Jesus do not provide us so much with answers as with meaning, which is far more important. We do not understand but yet we believe. We believe in order to understand. With the passion of Jesus, God immersed himself into the heart of the mystery of suffering. With the passion of Jesus, he has aligned himself with the poor, the oppressed, the powerless and all who suffer in the world. Through them he makes himself present to us and among them he is to be found. He is not a god like Superman. Rather, 'He was oppressed and was afflicted, yet he opened not his mouth; he was like a lamb that is led to the slaughter' (Isaiah 54:7). He is the suffering servant, a man of sorrows, the God of love, the God of Jesus Christ.

Prayer:

'Lord Jesus Christ, in times of suffering and sorrow, never allow me to descend into self-pity. Help me to unite my suffering with yours for it is in your cross that I share. With you I offer my struggle for the love of you and all humanity. Amen.'

The Mystery of Suffering and Death

The cross continues to be the primary symbol of Christianity because it expresses the hidden but effective victory of love over evil, sin and death. With the death of Jesus comes hope that is offered to all his followers who suffer. Be it from events over which we have no control such as sickness, famine or bereavement, or from suffering that has been self-inflicted as a result of our own sin, the love of God is there offering the chance of transformation and change. St Paul puts it well when he asks us never to forget that we possess the Spirit of him who rose Jesus from the dead and that no matter how much we are surrounded by darkness, we will never be alone, for 'These are the trials through which we triumph by the power of him who loved us' (Romans 8:37). Jesus suffers with us and for us and he has promised that we will share in the victory that he has won for us. His death and resurrection have broken the power of evil so that it cannot have the last word in human history, no matter how dark that history becomes. Jesus Christ is the suffering servant who willingly suffers out of love for his brothers and sisters. By showing the Father's love for us, Jesus loved us to the end and died preaching the message of love that he had lived all his life, 'Greater love has no one than this, that a person lay down their life for their friends' (John 13:1; 15:13).

If the mystery of suffering is part of God's plan of love for us then it is consoling to know that Jesus, God's total gift of himself, was not spared from it. As has often been said, we will never walk down any road of human suffering but we will find his footsteps already there before us. We will never fully understand why we suffer. The process of finding meaning in suffering can be helped by simply accompanying each other in the search for meaning. It involves us being people of compassion, a word that means 'to suffer with'. For the lover of Christ crucified, it involves being with another person in their space of pain and sharing their suffering in a way that reassures them 'you are not alone'.

We will need to wait until the next world before we understand and know the answer to the question 'Why? Why me? Why do I have to suffer like this?' Nevertheless we also believe that the dark moments of our lives can be turning points and moments of grace. They can be moments that awaken us out of our selfishness and open our eyes to those who are suffering more than we are. When we look back at our experiences of suffering, with God's grace, we may recognise ourselves among those the Lord referred to as 'branches that bear fruit he prunes to make it bear even more' (John 15:2).

If we avoid bitterness and resentment, our sufferings have the capacity to transform us into people of greater humility and draw us closer to one another and to the Lord.

A few thoughts on the moment Jesus died. The first time I saw someone die was at a hospital where I was called in the early hours to minister to a man who was seriously ill. His family were around his bed and it was a very emotional experience for them as they walked with their dad on the last few steps of his journey in life. As he lay dying, the words of Jesus from the cross echoed in our minds as he prepared to make his final act of entrustment to the Father, 'Into your hands I commend my Spirit' (Luke 23:46). They remind us that eventually we will have to let go of everything and everyone until at last all we are left with is our faith in God's love for us.

When that moment comes for all of us, all that will remain is the belief that God is there waiting for us with open arms of forgiveness and welcome to receive us into his company forever. When we think about it, we are preparing for that moment all our lives. God's grace invites us to let go of everything and everyone that comes before him. The experience of life is one long process of learning to trust God more. In learning to trust, we are freed from our attachments to false gods and in time discover who we truly are. St Teresa of Avila, who herself was no stranger to intense suffering, once wrote, 'A person can bear all things provided they possess Christ Jesus dwelling within them as their friend and affectionate guide'.

In life, as in death, we pray that we may live each day those beautiful words of trust in God, 'Father, Into your hands I commend my Spirit'.

Prayer:

> 'Lord Jesus, out of love for us, you embraced every possible aspect of our human experience in order to bring your saving love close. Deepen our trust that you are near even when we feel that you are not. Be there especially in our trials, our sadness, our

loneliness and bereavement. Give us hope, healing and forgiveness. Lead us to fresh and green pastures where you will refresh us and give us peace. In our pain, help us never to forget others who suffer, especially those who carry a heavier cross. Amen.'

'HE DESCENDED INTO HELL'

When the Creed says that Jesus 'descended into hell' it is saying that Jesus really died and suffered the effects of death that every human being has to suffer. Jesus died and went to 'Hades' or the name given to the place where all the dead have to go. The Church teaches that Jesus also had a mission to perform when he got there. He had come to free the just who had gone before him. His love for humanity was so powerful that it was not just the living who would benefit from his offer of salvation. It was a gift offered to every human being that ever lived. This was the will of God so that the dead would hear the voice of the Son of God and those who heard and accepted it would live (cf. 1 Peter 3:19).

This is the great mystery the Church celebrates on Holy Saturday. It is the time when all believers keep prayerful vigil around the tomb of Jesus and await what he promised. When we speak of Jesus 'descending into hell' we acknowledge not only a hell after death but the possibility of a 'living hell' for people on earth. We often hear of people who have suffered greatly who know the pain of isolation and the feeling of being abandoned by everyone and maybe even by God. Maybe we have been in that space ourselves at some stage. Maybe we are there now. If this is true then the descent of Jesus into hell is a window of hope for all. It means that Jesus on the cross experienced the 'living hell' of being in agony and feeling utterly abandoned by everyone including God his Father. This is why he cried out those words that so many have made their own at the darkest moments of life, 'My God, my God, why have you forsaken me?' (Mark 15:34). These words of Jesus were spoken from a space of utter desolation and emptiness. It is into that space of abandonment that God's love has gone in order to offer hope to everyone in history who would find themselves in that space too.

The descent of Jesus into hell reminds us of how the love of God works and teaches us more of its depths and heights. Such is the love of God that it is prepared to suffer and go to the furthest possible extremes in order to offer hope and salvation to anyone who needs it. Therefore there is no situation from which God cannot draw a greater good. There is no suffering that he cannot transform into a path leading to him. For this reason, the hope of the resurrection is offered to all.

Finally, the 'descent of Christ into hell' speaks to us about the importance of Holy Saturday in the liturgy. In the parish during Holy Week, maybe we don't give enough thought as to what it means or we may see it simply as a short day that links Good Friday and Easter Sunday, allowing us to make further preparations for the Bank Holiday weekend.

Holy Saturday is about waiting patiently, keeping vigil. It is a time for silence and for deep reflection on what we have celebrated on Good Friday. It teaches us that it is not possible to go directly from Good Friday to Easter Sunday without patiently living through a time of mourning, waiting and hoping. Holy Saturday tells us that difficulties are sure to come our way but that very often the place we are called to be is there with the mess, facing our issues with courage and staying put. As Padre Pio advised his fellow Christians, 'Place all your trust in God and don't be too eager to be set free from your present state. Let the Holy Spirit act within you'.[1] Holy Saturday invites us to live through our troubles bravely and not to run away

---

1   From a letter on Palm Sunday, 29 March 1914, to Raffaelina Cerase, taken from *Correspondence*, Vol. II.

from them. It is hope that gives us the strength to do so, a hope that God will grant us new life in his own time and in his own way. It is the hope that comes with facing up to whatever needs facing, believing that nothing has been left untouched by the power of God that makes all things new. A better day may seem like a long way off but 'Having this hope for what we cannot yet see, we are able to wait for it with persevering confidence' (Romans 8:25). This is a hope that will not deceive us for it has been placed in our hearts by God. It is his gift that leads us forward out of the darkness and silence of Holy Saturday into the new dawn and joy of Easter Sunday.

Prayer:

'God Our Father, such was the power of your love that death could not contain your love for humanity. The Spirit of Jesus your Son who had given his life for all, reached back and offered that love to all who had ever lived. May our love reflect something of yours and reach out to all people, in all places and at all times. Amen.'

'On the Third Day
he Rose Again'

Introduction

The Gospels tell us that on the third day after his death, Jesus rose. What an extraordinary statement! What a message to proclaim! Yet for us as Christians, it is the bedrock of everything we believe in. As St Paul reminds us, 'If Christ has not been raised, then our preaching is in vain and your faith is in vain' (1 Corinthians 15:14). From the Gospel texts, the resurrection of Jesus was a real experience that touched the disciples deeply. Jesus' human body that was battered and tortured on the cross was transformed by the power of the Holy Spirit and raised from the dead. After the resurrection, Jesus' body bore the marks of his crucifixion and death. He invited Thomas to come and touch his wounded side (cf. John 20:27). He asked for some food and ate it before their eyes (cf. Luke 24:42). In this sense he showed us that there was a continuity between the Jesus they knew before the resurrection and the way he was now. However, he was also different. He came through closed doors (cf. John 20:19). He went unrecognised by his followers (cf. Luke 24:16). In some way his glorified body was transformed and different than before.

Looking back on over two thousand years of testimony and belief in the resurrection, it is not hard to see why most Christians have been convinced that if Jesus had died rejected by the Jews, executed by the Romans and deserted by his followers, without anything occurring beyond that, then the movement that is Christianity would not have got off the ground. But very soon after the crucifixion of Jesus, the disciples began to spread the word: 'Jesus is not dead, he is alive'.

The bold belief in the resurrection meets the same opposition today as it did two thousand years ago albeit in different ways. There were many doubts then and there are many doubts now. However, the biggest challenge to those who disbelieve must surely be the witness and faith of millions of people down through the centuries who have come together each week to proclaim 'He is risen', and who celebrate the Spirit of Jesus as being ever present to them. These people of faith have spread and grown to become the greatest communion or family the world has ever known, the family of the Church. Can so many people be wrong?

Prayer:

'It is truly right that with full hearts, minds and voices we should praise the unseen God, the all powerful father, and his only Son, Our Lord Jesus Christ.

This is the night when Christians everywhere washed clean of sin and freed from all defilement, are restored to grace and grow together in holiness. Father, how wonderful your care for us! How boundless your merciful love! To ransom a slave you gave away your Son.'[1]

---

1   From 'The Exsultet'; Easter Vigil.

Easter Sunday Christians

The basis of the faith of the early Church was that, because Jesus had been raised by the Father, his person, his message and his whole way of life had been vindicated. He had put himself on the line for the outcast, the despised, the guilt ridden, the oppressed of body and mind, the poor and those in most need of help. His death followed the spilling of his blood that he shed in order to remain faithful to his convictions and commitments. With the resurrection of Jesus, hope was restored for all those he had loved. It truly was and is good news. The resurrection of Jesus was a continuation of the one saving event that the Father had done through Jesus and continues to do for us. With the crucifixion and death of Jesus came the gravest injustice ever committed when goodness itself was nailed to a cross by the powers of evil and sin. For a moment it seemed that humanity was lost to despair forever. However, God had other things in mind and was not prepared to let this happen, for love can never die. The Father transformed the life of Jesus, killed by sinners, into God's way of setting us free and saving us from anything that would dehumanise us through guilt, oppression and degrading poverty. While evil still abounds in the world, the back of sin has been broken; it has no definitive power any more and is doomed to pass away.

When we consider how best to deal with the many injustices we see around us, it is good for us to remember this. If we are successful in our campaigns or protests against injustice, then the fruit borne has come as a result of God's action through us. Faith in the resurrection is the fountain that gives birth to a policy of non-violence; a policy that was so effectively adopted by people like Ghandi, Oscar Romero, Nelson Mandela and of course by the Lord himself. Witness to the resurrection does not try to overcome adversaries by defeating them. It tries rather to win people over and invites them to friendship and conversion. Faith in the resurrection of Jesus bears with it a love that St Paul described as 'patient, kind and enduring all things' (cf. 1 Corinthians 13:4ff). Yet an Easter faith is one that is also courageous and inspires us to speak out when it is necessary. It is not a feeling or a mood. It is a gift that comes from our God who has entered into the darkness of this world in order to carry there the light of peace, hope and love. One man who lived in the last century and who lived as a witness to the resurrection was Archbishop Oscar Romero. He found himself at the end of the 1970s entrusted with the task of leading a Church that was undergoing a severe persecution at the hands of a corrupt government. Hundreds of innocent El Salvadorians were tortured and killed. Romero's response was one that typified an Easter Sunday Christian whose cry to his people was one of 'Alleluia!' In the face of violence, he refused any approach or words that smacked of violence as a response to violence. The only violence he spoke of and witnessed to was what he called a 'violence of love'. Offering the killers forgiveness and fellowship was an approach that recoiled their evil ways back on themselves in a manner that invited them to repentance. He carried the light of the Gospel into the very heart of the darkness that surrounded him. His humility made him realise that his own life could never be as important as the telling of the Good News to the poor and he gained strength from the words of Jesus he read in the Gospel of St John: 'Unless a grain of wheat falls to the ground and dies, it remains but a single grain; but if it dies it yields a rich harvest' (12:24). Shortly before his assassination he spoke of the possibility of an attempt on his life. Filled with Easter faith he replied:

> As a Christian, I do not believe in death without resurrection: if they kill me, I will rise again in the Salvadorian people ... May my death, if accepted

by God, be for the freedom of my people and a
witness to hope for the future. A bishop will die,
but the Church of God, which is the people, will
never perish.[2]

God was very good to us when he blessed us with the example
of Easter Christians like Oscar Romero.

We are also inspired to live our Easter faith by others closer
to home. Many of our grandparents, our parents and our
friends stand out as examples of people whose Easter faith has
sustained them through times of worry and difficulty. In their
own unique way, these people have given us fresh hope in the
promises of the Lord when it seemed that despair had won the
day. I think in particular of the men and women who have
suffered the trauma of the death of a child or the death from
illness of a family member. We think of people who have had
relatives murdered or affected by suicide. For these people their
faith has been purified and their hope undimmed as they
prayerfully sit and wait by the graves of their loved ones on
Patron day and on different occasions during the year. Tragedy
has not destroyed them as they cling to the promises of him in
whom they believe: 'I am the resurrection and the life. Anyone
who believes in me, even though they die, yet will they live and
whoever lives and believes in me will never die' (John 11:25).

As the resurrection is a source of hope in death so too is it a
fountain of hope in life. Many of us struggle not only with loss
through death but also with loss in life: the loss of innocence
through abuse, the betrayal of trust that has left us emotionally
scarred or some painful experience that is burned into our
memory. The resurrection of Jesus is a powerful reminder that
we have been given a share in his victory over all hurt and

---

2   From *Homilias*, Vol. IV, 11 May 1978.

injustice. Jesus too was innocent and yet he suffered more than anyone. The hatred and violence that he absorbed onto himself did not ferment into bitterness but instead was changed into forgiveness, healing and love. He was a victim of all the cruelties of man's inhumanity to man. Yet he did not allow it to control or destroy him. His curse became a blessing that he freely shared with the whole world. We think of the many times that the prayer life of the Church has sustained and nurtured the hope of the resurrection in the hearts of her members. We think of the Easter vigil in particular and every Mass we celebrate where we proclaim our faith in Christ's resurrection and his return to us in glory. We think of the power and strength that God makes present to us through his word; forever encouraging us, guiding us, inspiring us and chiding us when necessary. God's people who suffer most have come to know that truly, 'God is close to the broken hearted and those whose spirit is crushed he will save' (Psalm 34:18). Through their lives of prayer, the risen Christ's gentle spirit of mercy touches those who are hurting and speaks to bruised and broken hearts. We think of the many candles lit each day in our parish Churches under the careful watch of the Sacred Heart or Our Lady. We think of the people who light them and why they do. We think of the hope that fills their hearts, a hope that these burning candles symbolise. 'It is a hope that will not deceive us, because the love of God has been poured into our hearts' (Romans 5:5). We think of the many people of faith and goodwill who gather signatures, who march the streets peacefully in fair weather and foul, for a cause that is just. These are just some examples of people for whom the resurrection is not something that comes after death but something that is real and whose effects are coming to bear in the here and now. After all, did not the angel who greeted the disciples at the empty tomb say to them, 'Why do you seek the living among the dead?' (Luke 24:5).

Prayer:

'*Father all powerful and ever living God,*
we do well always and everywhere to give you thanks
through Jesus Christ Our Lord.
In him a new age has dawned, the long reign of sin
is ended, a broken world has been renewed and we
are once again made whole.
The joy of the resurrection renews the whole world
while the choirs of heaven sing forever to your glory.'[3]

---

3   Preface IV: Mass for Easter.

'He Ascended into Heaven and is Seated at the Right Hand of the Father'

Introduction

Karl Marx was a famous figure who found religion hard to take. He once famously described it as 'the opium of the people'. For him, faith was impossible when he saw the effect it had on people, especially the poor. For Marx and several others like him, faith in God disempowered people from taking responsibility for their own lives, making them hope that somehow the next life would be better and would make up for the misery of the present moment. Christians reminded him of the people who witnessed the Ascension of Jesus and who remained standing and looking into another world instead of concentrating on this one. Marx's criticisms remind us that our faith must have a social aspect and be relevant for life as we experience it here on earth. It must speak to our situations in life in the here and now. We must not spend our lives waiting for heaven.

Prayer:

'Loving Father, help me to spend my heaven doing good on earth.
Never allow me to be distracted from seeing you in my brothers and sisters that you call me to serve and love. Amen.'

Ascension

The command of the angels to the disciples at the Ascension to cast their gaze once again towards earth (cf. Acts 1:11) is a command to Christians for all times and seasons. It is an invitation from God to look once again into our world where God has made his home.

Christianity is a flesh and blood religion. It is raw, physical and earthy. God's presence comes in the great wonder of God becoming a human being and speaking to us directly from our human experience. The message of Jesus' life was that we cannot bypass the physical to reach the spiritual. Indeed Jesus shocked and scandalised many of his religious peers with his contact with the blind, lepers, prostitutes and the like. In the Jewish mind, contact with such people excluded one from religious worship with the community. His biggest critics claimed that because he did this, he could not possibly be from God because God would never be found in the company of such people, never mind have any physical contact with them. But Jesus went even further. By embracing humanity in all its beauty and brokenness, he transformed it by his touch that was characterised by healing, forgiveness, inclusion and peace. In this way he glorified humanity taking it to a new and higher level of existence. The ascension of Jesus celebrates this mystery and celebrates humanity being assumed to a new dignity by God.

With his ascension, Jesus is present to us in a different but no less real way where we are invited to recognise him 'by faith not by sight' (2 Corinthians 5:7). In this new way of being, the Spirit of the risen Christ fills the world and fulfils his promise that he will be 'With us always until the end of time' (Matthew 28:20). With this mystery of faith, Jesus never ceases to be there for us, embracing us in a new intimacy and offering us the same gifts he did to those we read about in the Gospels. The gifts he offered, the love he shared was all part of a wonderful plan that had been in the mind of God for all eternity. It was the dream of 'the kingdom of God' where everything would be united together and united in God. It was for this that Jesus had come. He had come down from heaven in order to raise us up to heaven with him. The ascension is a foretaste that God's dream will one day be fulfilled because now, in Jesus, God has 'United all things in him, things in heaven and things on earth' (Colossians 1:20). With Jesus' ascension comes the hope that ours will follow. Jesus' glorified body is like what ours will become. Like him and with him we will one day be beyond death, pain and suffering. There, the Lord's heartfelt desire will be accomplished at last: 'Father I want those you have given me to be with me where I am' (John 17:24).

Like the resurrection, the ascension is a mystery that we share in now. If we are living the Gospel then we are already in that place where Jesus is. This ascension into glory of our bodies, souls, minds, hearts and spirits has already begun. With the life, death, resurrection and ascension of Jesus, God the Father has raised us to a new level and made this possible.

Prayer:

'God Our Father, make us joyful in the ascension of your Son, Jesus Christ.
May we follow him into the new creation, for his ascension is our glory and our hope.
Grant this through the same Christ Our Lord. Amen.'[1]

---

1   Opening Prayer: Mass of the Ascension.

'Seated at the Right Hand of the Father'

The words '… and is seated at the right hand of the Father' that we profess in the Creed speak to us of the authority of Jesus as Lord and Saviour. In the Jewish mind, for someone to sit at the right hand of someone in authority was symbolic of sharing in that same authority; 'The Lord says to my Master, sit on my right hand until I make your enemies your footstool' (Psalm 110:1). We still use a similar expression when we refer to someone being 'his right-hand man'. As the eternal priest, Jesus is the highest authority who intercedes for humanity with the Father, shares his authority and who assures us of the permanent outpouring of the Holy Spirit. That is why St John prays in the Book of revelation, 'Worthy are you O Lord to take the scroll and to open its seals; for you were slain and by your blood you ransomed men and women for God from every tribe and tongue and people and nation' (Revelation 5:9). As such he is beyond reproach or compromise and his authority is forever. This is our faith; this is the faith of the Church universal. Jesus is Lord!

Prayer:

'Loving Father, draw us ever deeper into the mystery and beauty of your Son Jesus who came not to be served but to serve and to give his life as a ransom for many. Amen.'

'FROM THENCE HE SHALL COME TO JUDGE THE LIVING AND THE DEAD'

This article of the Creed brings us face to face with the statement of belief in the second coming of Jesus Christ at the end of time. This is a belief the Church contemplates in a special way during the first half of advent and each time we celebrate Mass; 'Christ has died, Christ has risen, Christ will come again' (The Mystery of Faith). Here we ponder the mystery that 'God has fixed a day on which he will judge the world' (Acts 17:31). When this day will be, no one knows. It could be in our lifetime or maybe thousands of years from now. Whenever it is, we will one day stand with our naked selves before the Lord, with hands empty and with no hiding place. Then 'Everything is uncovered and open to the eyes of the One to whom we must give an account of ourselves' (Hebrews 4:13). This article of faith invites us to consider 'That day when we shall see you as You really are' (Eucharistic Prayer III). It encourages us not to be afraid but rather to be ready: 'You do not know the day when your Master is coming. Therefore you must stand ready because the Son of Man is coming at an hour you do not expect' (Matthew 24:41). But then a question comes to our minds. What will this moment be like? Will it be terrifying?

When we think about God as judge, it is not surprising that we think of all the human images of courts, judges, punishments etc. and imagine that heavenly judgement will be something similar. Misunderstandings of God's judgement lead to the familiar question that we have all heard and perhaps even asked ourselves: 'If God is so merciful how could he possibly send anyone to hell?' Not surprisingly, thoughts of this kind of judgement have turned many a human heart cold with fear.

The key to this article of the Creed is the pronoun 'he'. HE will come to judge the living and the dead. This 'he' is the Jesus who would not cast the first stone, who had tenderness for those who had failed, who did not despise sinners but who dined with them. Possibly we are so familiar with these Gospel stories of God's mercy that we fail to realise just how much potential they have to change our lives. The attitude of Jesus to those who had failed, appalled the pious and enraged the authorities. In the Gospel of Luke, Simon the Pharisee could not understand how Christ would allow a woman as notorious as Mary Magdalen to approach him, much less anoint him (7:36-50). Yet Jesus loved Mary and was aware of her love, accepting her and forgiving her sins: 'Much is forgiven her because she has loved much' (v.47). Our hope is that on the day of our judgement the same words Jesus spoke about Mary will also be spoken about us. Those who have been merciful themselves will have no fear of judgement. If we have loved much in this life then forgiveness from God will be abundant.

So we can let go of the idea of an angry God whom we will meet on judgement day. If people are in hell they are there not of God's doing. He has allowed them to have what they really want, for hell is a self-made prison. If we choose to reject love, to refuse forgiveness, then we have put ourselves in a hell of our own making. If we have lived lives of selfishness and destruction without repentance, then we come before God as we are and he accepts us as such.

In the scene of the final judgement in Chapter 25 of St Matthew's Gospel, we see a perfect example of how we all will be judged on love. 'As long as you did it to the least of my brothers and sisters, you did it to me' (v.40). Here, the last judgement is described as the angels separating sheep and goats on the last day, the sheep on their way to eternal life and the goats to damnation (25:32-34). It is interesting to notice from this passage that it is not God who decides who are sheep and who are the goats. They are as they are, already. God's angels merely separate them. In this sense, judgement is in the here and now. We do not have to wait until we are dead to know where we stand before God. If we live in him, doing our best to be people of love, peace and forgiveness, listening attentively to God's word in the Scriptures, in the voice of the Church and living accordingly; if we live in a spirit of prayer and respect for all humanity then we know where we stand with our God. At our judgement we will be judged on how we have responded to the least of our brothers and sisters who live in our midst, for Christ presents himself to us in these people. If we have been merciful to them then we have nothing to fear: 'As long as you did it to the least of these brothers and sisters of mine you did it to me' (25:40). In the words of St John of the Cross, 'At the evening of life, we shall all be judged on love'. Faith and hope will have brought us through time but will leave us at the doorstep of eternity. Only love will carry us inside. On the day of our judgement the God we will face will be one who will be no stranger to us, for as Job tells us in the Old Testament, 'He whom I shall see will take my part: my eyes will be gazing on no stranger' (19:27).

If, however, we have been deaf to the cry for help from the poor and have failed to respond to them, then we have already brought judgement down on ourselves. By ignoring the poor and the weakest, we have ignored Christ. Even then, God is not like a cold judge passing sentence upon us. Rather throughout our lives he is like a distraught lover, desperate to save the one he loves who is lost. He is like the Father of the prodigal son who goes out every day to scan the horizon to wait in the hope that someday his child will come back to his house. God cajoles and pleads; he entices but never forces us to open the door of our hearts. He stands ready and waiting to enter but never without invitation: 'Behold, I stand at the door and knock. If anyone hears my voice and opens the door, I will come in' (Revelation 3:20).

Prayer:

'Lord Jesus, give me the grace never to lose the courage to ask for your mercy and forgiveness. Help me to pray with the good thief, "Jesus, remember me when you come into your kingdom". Let your cross be set up at my death bed. And let your lips say to me also, "Amen I say to you, today you will be with me in paradise". Amen.'

'I BELIEVE IN THE HOLY SPIRIT'

Moved by the Spirit

In the Scriptures, the Holy Spirit is represented or symbolised in the Old Testament by wind and breath (Genesis 1:2), oil (anointing of David, 1 Samuel 16:13), water (Ezekiel 47:1-12) and in the New Testament by a dove (Matthew 3:16), by water (John 4:10-14; 1 Corinthians 10:4), again by breath (cf. John 20:22) and by fire (Luke 1:17; Acts 2:3-4). All of these symbols convey that the Spirit brings with it the life of God.

When reading the Bible we immediately see the importance of the Holy Spirit in God's loving plan for the world. In only the second sentence of the Book of Genesis it is referred to as God's instrument for creating order and for bringing the world into being (cf. 1:2). When God decided to create humanity we are told that, 'The Lord God formed man from the soil of the ground and blew the breath of life into his nostrils, and man became a living being' (2:7). This very significant passage from God's word sets the scene for the role of the Holy Spirit that is consistently seen throughout the Old and New Testament.

The Holy Spirit is the 'Lord the giver of life' and is found wherever life exists. From every cell in our bodies to the breath in our lungs to the thoughts we think. The spirit is the life in every tree, in every fish, in every animal that lives. It is the spirit present in all creation that breathes and unites in a fine interdependent balance, helping creation to grow, to regenerate and to attain immortality. The hidden component in all living things is the Holy Spirit, who holds all things in being. At the Mass, the priest expresses this belief of the Church when he prays on behalf of the community present, 'All life, all holiness comes from you through your Son, Jesus Christ Our Lord, by the working of the Holy Spirit' (Eucharistic Prayer III).

The spirit that God breathed into Adam at the dawn of creation is the same spirit that Jesus breathed on his disciples at Pentecost. It is the same spirit that we have received and that sustains us. We live the 'spiritual life' when we live a life filled with the breath of God, a breath that fills all the cracks and depths of human existence. It is the Spirit of God that enables us to be moved when watching a film or reading a poem that makes us think again. It is the Spirit that leads us to feel alive knowing that someone loves us for who we are. It is the Spirit that erupts within us and lifts our minds and hearts to a world beyond ourselves when we stand watching the sun go down on a beautiful summers evening. It is the Spirit that moves us when we listen to a beautiful piece of music. It is the same Spirit that allows us to look at a new-born child and to exclaim, 'There must be a God!'

Prayer:

'Come Holy Spirit, renew your wonders in this our day as by a new Pentecost. That being one of mind and heart and steadfast in prayer with Mary, the Mother of Jesus, we may advance your divine kingdom of justice and peace, of truth and of love. Amen.'

We are Temples of the Holy Spirit

God has made us for himself and all our deepest desires remind us of that great truth. God has built us in a way that is forever calling us back to him. Our human nature is open and turned towards God in a way that allows him to communicate to us and we to him. This is possible only through the gift of the Holy Spirit. It is God's gift of himself and it is a gift that is ever present to us. What God gives out of his goodness he will never take back. St Paul reminds us of our great dignity as vessels of the Holy Spirit where he tells us 'As you are children, God has sent into our hearts, the Spirit of his Son crying 'Abba' Father' (Galatians 4:6).

In his letter to the Ephesians, St Paul puts before his audience their possession of this awesome mystery when he prays, 'Glory to him whose power working within us can do infinitely more than we can ever ask for or imagine' (3:20). Because this is true, it is the Holy Spirit that prompts us to pray, an exercise the old catechism defined as a lifting of the mind and heart to God. When the Spirit of God is alive in our hearts, prayer is something that we want to do and need to do: we feel the need to come before him and to render thanks and praise for all his gifts. God's initiative and desire is that he lives with us and in us with whom he is well pleased (cf. Luke 2:14). God has made his home in us and delights in doing so. He simply asks in return that we recognise this and that we make our home in him too; 'Remain in me as I am in you' (John 15:4). Each time we pray is an encounter with the Most Blessed Trinity who dwells in the depths of our being. This is the foundation stone of all contemplative prayer that seeks God in reflection and meditation. So important is the endeavour of every Christian to meet God in the mirror, so to speak, that many of the great saints of the Church point to the danger of not doing so.

St Augustine was one such person who desperately sought God in external things and places before he found him in a place he hadn't expected. In his *Confessions*, he sums up brilliantly the drama that took place in his heart, 'Late have I loved you O beauty so ancient and true, late have I loved you! For behold you were within me, and I outside. I sought you outside and my ugliness fell upon those lovely things that you have made. You were with me and I was not with you'.[1] As St Augustine was to discover, God is always at home, closer to myself than I am. If this is true then the question arises, 'If God is fully present to me, am I present to myself?' To the extent that we are, then we experience God. Where people like Saint John of the Cross, Teresa of Avila and Therese of Lisieux differ from us is not in the fact that they were loved more by God than the rest of us. Rather their greatness lay in their capacity always to be aware of the present moment where God was with them. We on the other hand tend to be out of the house quite a bit, distant from ourselves and hence from God (but never God from us).

The Holy Spirit leads us on an inner journey as well as on an external one. Prayer is a time of being still and knowing that he is God and that his presence fills every cell of our bodies. In coming before God in prayer, words are not always necessary. Indeed sometimes they get in the way. Even when we feel dry and do not know how to pray as we ought, 'the Spirit himself intercedes with sighs too deep for words' (Romans 8:26). Thus, as Jesus described it in St John's Gospel, the Spirit is a living water welling up in us to eternal life (cf 4:10-14). Prayer inspired by the Holy Spirit is a time of intimacy with God when we return to that inner sanctuary we call our truest self. It is here where we guard what is most sacred to us and here that we

---

1 Book 10, 27.

encounter ourselves as we truly are and God as he really is. It is here to this sanctuary that we must go in order to know him. Otherwise we run the risk of knowing about him rather than really knowing him and experiencing his love. As St John tells us, 'Eternal life is this: to know you, the only true God and Jesus Christ whom you have sent' (17:3).

May we return time and time again to that sacred place in our hearts where God is waiting to meet us, where we will know him and know ourselves. There in that sacred space may we draw out from the well of God's love what we pour out in public for all to see.

Prayer:

'Loving God, help me to believe what you say is true. Help me to believe that my heart is your dwelling place. Help me to return there often where I can meet you and my true self. Amen.'

The Holy Spirit in the Community

The Holy Spirit unites us with God and God with us. It is the spirit who sets us apart at our baptism for service and who absorbs us into the life, death and resurrection of Jesus Christ. The Spirit is also the means by which we have a bond with a fellow Christian by which we recognise them as a brother or sister. It is the bond between all Christians that leads us to live the Gospel not as individuals but together as a community of believers. It is what helps us recognise in these times that we need one another for support in order to live out the values of the Gospel in a world that sometimes opposes them. Theologians use the beautiful word 'communion' to describe this mysterious yet powerful concept of being united to God and to our fellow Christians. It describes this bond of the spirit that creates unity and togetherness. In fact at Mass, we receive Holy Communion as the great sign of our communion with the Blessed Trinity and our communion with one another as Church. We receive communion because we are in communion.

As well as individual Christians being the bearers of the Spirit, so does the Spirit dwell in the people of God collectively. It was to the community that the Holy Spirit was given at Pentecost when the Apostles were gathered with Our Lady at prayer in the upper room (cf. Acts 2:1ff). From then on the Holy Spirit has always been present to the Church as the people of God and has been the force behind the work of God that she has carried out over the centuries. We are indebted to St Luke for his writings on the workings of the Holy Spirit in the plan of God. Luke is also believed to have been the source of the Acts of the Apostles. For Luke, Jesus is the bearer of the Holy Spirit that he receives at his baptism at the hands of John, 'The heavens opened and the Holy Spirit descended on him in a physical form, like a dove. And a voice came from heaven, "You are my Son; today I have Fathered you"' (Luke 3:22). Jesus is anointed with the Spirit and empowered by it. In the synagogue in Nazareth where he had been brought up, Jesus publicly stated this when he got up to speak and read from the Scriptures: 'The Spirit of the Lord is upon me, for he has anointed me to bring good news to the poor. He has sent me to proclaim liberty to captives, to give sight to the blind, to let the oppressed go free and to proclaim a year of favour from the Lord' (cf. Isaiah 61:1-2; Luke 4:18).

In the Acts of the Apostles, Luke draws a parallel between the coming of the Holy Spirit upon Jesus at his baptism and the coming of the Holy Spirit upon the community of believers.

Only when the community had received the Holy Spirit could they be witnesses to the Gospel in the world. As with Jesus' ministry, the Church now received the same Spirit and the same mandate to carry on the mission of Jesus until the end of time. As with Jesus, the Church is now the bearer of the Holy Spirit that empowers her to perform the same works as Jesus did with the same effects. As St Ambrose once wrote, 'The Lord has willed his disciples to possess a tremendous power: that his lowly servants accomplish in his name all that he did when he was on earth'.[2]

God has placed his own power at our fingertips. But as in the life of Jesus, it is a power given only for the betterment of his people and the glory of God. It is a power to love, to forgive, to heal, to preach and to tell the Good News, all in his name. This is a power that we possess collectively, not as individuals. This is why every Christian is called to think and worship with the Church community and not independent of it. No one individual possesses the entire truth. This resides in the community where the Spirit of God has chosen to dwell.

Prayer:

'Come Holy Spirit, live in us,
with God the Father and the Son,
and grant us your abundant grace to sanctify and
make us one.

'May mind and tongue made strong in love,
Your praise throughout the world proclaim,
And may that love within our hearts,
Set fire to others with its flame.'[3]

---

2   *De Poenitentia I*, 15: PL 16, 479.
3   From the Office of Readings; Opening hymn; Prayer during the Day.

The Gifts of the Holy Spirit

God uses a community that is brimming with his spirit to draw others to him and to share his life. The Holy Spirit is the agent by which God introduces people to the life of the Trinity that he wishes us to be part of. With the Spirit, God prepares us for the life he wishes us to have and goes out to meet us with his grace. It is the Spirit of God who does for us what we are unable to do for ourselves; namely to mould us into a community composed of people of every background and circumstance. As it moulds us into the body of Christ so too does the Spirit transform the gifts of bread and wine we offer at the Eucharist and change them into the Body and Blood of Christ. We then in turn receive 'this life giving bread' and 'this saving cup' (Eucharistic Prayer III). Just as many grains of wheat go to make one loaf of bread, so too we, though many, are one Body in Christ.

It is the Holy Spirit who kneads us together as a community to form a family who are called to be his witnesses in the world. Because this is true, it highlights the importance of all communities being places where the fruits of the Holy Spirit are allowed to flourish. The Holy Spirit is the giver of gifts not only to individual Christians but also to the Community.

Traditionally, the Church has described the seven gifts of the Holy Spirit as being *wisdom* (to recognise the ways and things of God); *understanding* (to penetrate the mysteries of faith); *counsel* (to choose and discern what is God's will); *fortitude* (to stand firm in the cause of virtue and truth); *knowledge* (to discern the difference between good and evil); *piety* (to faithfully practice and live our faith) and *fear of the Lord* (which inspires us with a respect for God and all he has made). These are the sevenfold gifts of the Spirit that manifest themselves in the fruits of the Spirit that should be seen in the life of every Christian and every faith community that he/she is part of: *love, joy, peace, patience, kindness, goodness, faithfulness, gentleness and self-control.*

Our parishes and communities are meant to be places that show forth the Spirit of Jesus Christ. As such they are called to possess a spirit of welcome to new members especially people who may be new to the parish. They are called to be communities where a spirit of joy and love resides among all the members and reaches out especially to those who are weakest and those most in need. They are to be places where everyone feels valued, where they have a voice, are appreciated and where they belong to a community they can call 'home'.

Prayer:

'God our Father, complete the work you have begun and keep the gifts of your Holy Spirit active in the hearts of your people. Make them ready to live his Gospel and eager to do his will.
May they never be ashamed to proclaim to all the world Christ crucified, living and reigning for ever and ever. Amen.'[4]

The Spirit of Joy

We rejoice in the closeness of our God. We rejoice in his friendship because as St Thomas Aquinas once wrote, 'friendship is the source of greatest joy'. It is with joy that we receive the Good News of God's lavish love like the shepherds did on that first Christmas night, announced by the angels, 'Do not be afraid. Look, I bring you news of great joy, a joy to be shared by the whole people' (Luke 2:10). St Luke, as we saw earlier, highlights the role of the Spirit in the ministry of Jesus and associates closely the gift of the Holy Spirit and the gift of

---

4   From the Rite of Confirmation.

joy that comes with it. Jesus himself is one who is filled with the Spirit and filled with joy, 'Filled with joy by the Holy Spirit, he said …' (Luke 10:21). St Paul in his letter to the Philippians urges all of us who are Christians to be joyful in the Lord and to rejoice in what God has done for us, 'Always be joyful then, in the Lord; I repeat, be joyful' (4:4). Elsewhere in his letter to the Romans he reminds us that 'The kingdom of God means peace and joy in the Holy Spirit' (14:17).

To be a sad and sombre Christian is a contradiction in terms for joy is the echo of God's life in us. As Mother Teresa once wrote, 'One filled with joy preaches without preaching'. Our Christian faith at its core is a life-affirming religion that gives thanks for the basic goodness of God's creation. At Eucharist we gather to praise God for the wonder of all he has made and for 'the wonder of my being'. Eucharist is our way of saying 'yes' to life and 'yes' to God. Yes! It is good to be here and good to be alive. Yes! It is true: 'God has made everything beautiful in its time' (Ecclesiastes 3:11).

For the Christian, even when we are suffering, the experience of joy is still possible. Our faith teaches us to view things from an eternal perspective and to remember that we are continuously being prepared for glory. The joy we experience by being close to God is a gift of the Holy Spirit and comes with loving God in response to God loving us. Being joyful Christians shows to the world the beautiful, enchanting and desirable face of God to whom we can confidently entrust our whole lives. In a world that desperately seeks happiness and contentment as an end in itself, we are reminded of what the joy of God is truly like by one who truly knew it: 'No one who has ever experienced it would ever exchange it for all the happiness in the world'.[5] The Gospel urges us to seek not the

5   From *Surprised By Joy*, C.S. Lewis.

joy of God but rather the God of joy. When we find him we
find joy.

Prayer:

'Father in heaven, see your people gathered in prayer,
Open to receive the Spirit's flame.
May it come to rest in our hearts
And disperse the divisions of word and tongue.
With one voice and one song
May we praise your name in joy and thanksgiving.
Grant this through Christ Our Lord. Amen.'[6]

---

6 Opening Prayer: Mass of Pentecost Sunday.

'I BELIEVE IN THE HOLY CATHOLIC CHURCH'

The Problem of Language

The meaning of the word 'Church' is difficult to define because the understanding of the word is changing all the time. Fifty years ago the word 'Church' was unanimously taken to mean the hierarchy of the Pope, the cardinals, bishops, priests, brothers and nuns. If a young man applied to join the seminary, the word quickly went around the parish that he was 'going for the Church'. Today, the meaning of the word has changed and broadened. An important model of the Church continues to be the hierarchical model but the word 'Church' now means so much more. The word 'Church' also means the people of God, it means the Body of Christ, it means the announcer of the Good News, to name but a few models of the Church that emerged after the Second Vatican Council. The language problem still arises in debate when one person or group uses the word 'Church' as meaning the hierarchical model and the other person or group in the debate understands the word differently. Numerous examples of this confusion have been seen over the years on TV, in newspaper columns and in other places where the life of the Church is discussed. The task to clarify what the Church is and is not is urgent so that we have a greater chance of learning from each other and growing in wisdom as God's people. We all need to understand the Church better and appreciate our calling to be part of it. What then or who is 'The Church'? What are we professing each Sunday when we stand and say together that we believe in the Church as One, Holy, Catholic and Apostolic? A look at where the word 'Church' comes from is a good place to begin.

Our word 'Church' comes from the German word *'Kirche'*, which in turn comes from the Greek word *'Kyriake'*, which literally means 'what belongs to the Lord'. Firstly then we must say that the Church is made up of a people who 'belong to the Lord'. The Church is, first and foremost, the community of people all over the world who believe in God and who profess Jesus Christ as their Lord and saviour. This faith we possess as a gift from God himself and we are enabled to profess it by the power of the Holy Spirit.

It is solely because of Our Lord Jesus Christ that the Church exists at all. The Church has no light other than Christ's. To borrow a favourite image from the Father's of the Church, the Church is called to shine the light and love of Christ onto the whole world. The Church is meant to be like the moon, with all its light reflected from her closeness to Christ just like the moon reflects all its light from the sun. Similar to how the moon shines its light away from itself, so too the Church points beyond itself to God and to his kingdom.

Let us now take a closer look at what the faith of our Church is saying when we profess that we believe in her as being One, Holy, Catholic and Apostolic.

Prayer:

'Loving God, at Pentecost, you sent the Holy Spirit upon your Church so that all Christians might understand one another in the universal language of faith and love.
Help all Christians to understand one another and in so doing, draw us closer together and closer to you. Amen.'

The Church is One and Catholic

Because the mission of the Church is to the whole world, it is fitting that people from all over the earth are part of her life. This is what we mean when we describe the Church as being universal and as Catholic. The Church embraces people of every nationality and culture. This universal dimension was there from the beginning. It was not as if a group of likeminded people of similar background came together to form the Church which then grew into a kind of worldwide federation. Symbolised by the gifts of tongues that the disciples received with the coming of the Holy Spirit at Pentecost, the infant Church gathered men and women from the four corners of the earth, the coming together of a diverse human family.

This essential nature of the Church remains today. As she was at Pentecost, so she continues to be. The Church continues to possess many diverse and rich cultural traditions and incorporates them into her life and liturgy. Within the unity of the people of God, many different peoples and cultures are gathered together. Among the Church's members there are different gifts, offices and ways of life. The great richness of this diversity is not opposed to the Church's unity but rather complements it. 'Unity in diversity' is a term that describes the Church but that finds its origin in the life of the Blessed Trinity: three distinct persons and yet one God. The Church is the people who have been gathered together by God and who share his life in the one spirit. We are a people who have been called into the same unity as that of the Father, the Son and the Holy Spirit.

Earlier in the chapter on the Holy Spirit, we looked at how God's Spirit in the Church did for us what we could not do for ourselves, that is to mould us into a community. This God does in a way *par excellence* at the Eucharist where we visibly express this coming together by gathering around the same Eucharistic table. There we celebrate the Church as being one for all because God, who wills her, is one for all. God has a catholic heart in the sense of it being wide and all encompassing. As Jesus revealed, 'There are many rooms in my Father's house' (John 14:2). There is a place in God's heart for everyone. The family of the Church brings together people who, from the point of view of their sensibilities and backgrounds, may not suit one another and perhaps seem to have very little in common. Yet there is a wonderful bond of something precious shared, a bond of love that has come from beyond us. This gift 'from beyond' is the love of he who died to reconcile the whole world. St Paul's letter to the Ephesians outlines the profound significance of the death of Jesus as being a sacrifice of love that has 'torn down the dividing wall of enmity that used to keep us apart' (2:14).

What is described here is the ideal but the reality is somewhat different. Despite the Lord's gift of unity to his Church she is still scandalously divided. Even within the same denominations there can be certain factions, right versus left, with each claiming to possess more of the truth than the other. For St Paul, the great evangelist and founder of Church communities, few issues concerned him more than the unity of the Churches. Indeed he felt compelled to write many of his letters and epistles in response to situations of division that had arisen where he had preached the Gospel. His first letter to the Corinthians is such an example. In the first chapter he states emphatically, 'Brothers and Sisters, I urge you in the name of Our Lord Jesus Christ, not to have factions among yourselves but for all to be in agreement in what you profess; so that you are perfectly united in your beliefs and judgements ... for you are saying "I belong to Paul", "I belong to Apollos" or "I belong to Cephas"' (cf. 1:10ff).

At Corinth in Paul's time, as it is today, it was disunity that was the enemy of the Church and that greatly weakened her message and mission. Paul reminded the people that it is Christ who is the head of the Church and all of us can be united only in him.

It is Christ who gave his life so that we could be one people and it was in his name that we were baptised. The Corinthians had fallen victim to a danger that has been forever present in the history of the Church, namely that of taking their eyes off the Lord. They had become distracted and were no longer watching Christ but one another. When this happens it quickly leads to a culture of suspicion and fear rather than love which tears at the heart of the Church's call to unity. We will always have tensions and moments of strain in the Church. However, the real test comes in how we respond when they arise. Being a Christian does not mean being best friends with everyone. It is easy to love someone whom we like and when we know that they like us. The real challenge is to love someone who irritates us or even dislikes us (cf. Luke 6:27-35). Yet this is what we are called to do in the Church. The call to reconciliation and forgiveness is not an optional extra part of our faith. It calls for repentance for ways in which we sought to score points over another person or group; repentance for ways in which we sought to convince ourselves or others that they were wrong and we were right. It calls us to see in everyone something of the spark of God.

The harvest is rich but the labourers are few. God is relying on us as his Church to create a world family where peace reigns. What he asks of us is simple, that we 'Love one another as I have loved you' (John 15:12). He has no feet, no hands but ours. Like a beggar that asks for bread he asks us to help make his dream come true. Will we?

Prayer:

'God Our Father, you are the creator of all the peoples on earth. The diversity of your people leads us to praise you with greater joy. In your eyes we are all part of the same family that you love dearly.
Give us a wide and deep heart so that we can embrace and love all peoples who are different to us. Take away the pride, prejudice and fear that keep us apart.
May we be one as you are one with the Son and the Holy Spirit, One God, forever and ever. Amen.'

The Church is Holy

To be holy does not mean to be pious. To be pious means to be outwardly observant of a life of faith and to have devotion to its practice. Hence when we describe someone as being 'holy' perhaps what we really mean is that they are pious. That is because we perceive them as regular Church goers, prayerful, devotional and respectful. The virtue of holiness means something different. To be holy means to be set apart, to be different. It is a call to a deep authenticity and fidelity on the part of every Christian. So too is it God's gift, given at baptism. There, we were anointed and set apart for service in God's kingdom here on earth. Baptism celebrates God's choice of us for a special task or vocation that only we can carry out. We are called by God to be 'holy', to be different, to be 'A chosen race, a royal priesthood, a holy nation and a people set apart' (1 Peter 2:9).

The Church then is holy because she is made up of people who are holy. We are the people who 'belong to the Lord' and

117

who have been called by him to join his company. From then on, our relationship with the world is not the same. We have a new mission entrusted to us, a vocation to love. At the Lord's request we are to be 'The salt of the earth and the light of the world, so that seeing our good works, others may give praise to our Father in heaven' (cf. Matthew 5:13-16). Jesus makes the Church holy because she is filled with his spirit and he has promised to be with us until the end of time. The Church is holy because of the Lord's choice to be with us always.

Side by side with God's presence in the Church is the presence of sin that comes from the hearts of her members. Sin dims the light of Christ that shines out to the world and decreases the effectiveness of her witness to the Gospel. Although Spirit filled, the Church is also a human institution and full of wounded and sinful humanity. It is still a pilgrim people and though it reflects the glory, truth and splendour of God, it also reflects the broken and sinful state of humanity. So although we rightly expect high standards from the Church, it comes as no surprise to discover it is riddled with the effects of original sin. The Christian people are in constant need of conversion from sin in order to remain faithful to their mission and mandate as entrusted to them by Christ.

The Church in Ireland is all too aware of the reality of failure when we look back on recent events. The scandals remind us to be ever alert to the presence of sin in our hearts and of how easy it is to lose sight of our God and his love. Yet the anger we may feel must also be accompanied by our responsibility not to pass quick or harsh judgements and to realise that none of us are immune from sin. The conversion and renewal of the Church is a process that includes everyone. I am responsible for the Church's holiness as are you. The call to 'Repent and Believe in the Gospel' (Mark 1:15) is always before us as individuals but so too is the call to conversion for our communities. All of us are responsible for the culture of our Church and for the authenticity of her relationships. It is not just about 'me'; it is about 'us'. We do not merely have a right but a duty to protest when we see or experience something that is not consistent with the Gospel message.

At times of crisis like the Church is living through now, we may not feel that we have been part of the problem but we are all part of the solution. The scandals have painfully taught us that we must work together in creating the proper environment in our communities, not of domination or power, but of service and love. We have learned of our need to listen to the call to conversion that sometimes comes from sources we do not expect. It means asking ourselves the question: Why do so many people reject the Church? Are they right to do so because of what they see? Is there truth in their criticisms? We must never again have the arrogance to think we are above reproach or that we are right and others are wrong. Criticisms need to be met not with defensiveness but with deep soul-searching, seeking always to grow in the truth. Jesus praised the faith of a Roman pagan in order to expose the lack of faith in his own disciples (cf. Luke 7:1-10). In the story, the call to conversion came from without. Today that call comes from within the Church and also from without. May we always listen to the truth wherever it comes from, for as Jesus said to Pilate, 'All who are on the side of truth listen to my voice' (John 18:37).

Prayer:

'God the Father of Our Lord Jesus Christ has freed you from sin, given you a new birth by water and the Holy Spirit and has welcomed you into his holy people.
He now anoints you with the chrism of salvation.

*As Christ was anointed Priest, Prophet and King, so
may you live always as a member of his body, sharing
everlasting life. Amen."*

The Church is Apostolic

The Twelve Apostles
The description of the Church as Apostolic comes from the part
the apostles played in the early Church. There is very strong
evidence in the Scriptures that out of all the many people who
followed Jesus, he took to himself twelve close associates who
were called apostles. They were his companions whom he
carefully chose following a whole night of prayer (cf. Luke 6:12).
They were the ones he chose to be with him to witness his
miracles, the parables, the transfiguration, the agony in the
garden, all the significant moments of his life. At the last supper
Jesus said to them, 'You are the men who have stood by me
faithfully in my trials, and now I confer a kingdom on you ...
you will sit on thrones to judge the twelve tribes of Israel' (Luke
22:28ff). This significant passage of Scripture indicates that the
apostles were to exercise some kind of leadership and authority
in the early years of the Church. So it proved to be. When there
were disputes or arguments about what the teachings of Jesus
meant, the matter was settled by seeing how true it was to the
teaching of the apostles (cf. Acts 2:42).

It has always been important for the Church to see herself in
direct continuity with the teaching of the apostles because they
themselves were taught by Jesus. Jesus gave them his spirit, the
Spirit of God (cf. John 20-22-23). The Holy Spirit is the
guarantee of the truth and in so far as the Church is motivated
by the Holy Spirit, it acts and speaks in that truth.

---

1   From the Rite of Baptism; Anointing with Chrism.

Prayer:

'Lord Jesus, you choose the twelve apostles after a night of prayer to the Father. Thank you for their example. Thank you also for the mercy you showed them when they failed. May we enjoy this same gift and be inspired by their preaching. Amen.'

Bishops: Successors of the Apostles

The apostles, special people as they were because of their selection by the Lord, were mere mortals like the rest of us. Some of them, like the apostle James, were executed soon after they began their life of preaching the Good News. Others began to grow older and to be more in demand as the Church began to grow in the places where the apostles had visited and preached. It was not long before the realisation grew that there needed to be a body of fellow Christians who would carry on the work and ministry of the apostles. This body of men became known as '*episkopoi*' (a word that means 'overseers' or 'guardians') and eventually in the Western world they became known as bishops. As the twelve apostles were a college or a fixed group, so too would be the college of bishops who succeeded them. They were to have specific responsibility for the local Church where they ministered and the universal Church that they also served. Matters of their own local Church or Diocese were not their sole concern. They also had responsibility for the Church worldwide. Most importantly, they were figures of unity in the family of the Church on earth.

Prayer:

Loving Father, I pray for all the bishops of the world and especially the bishop of our Diocese. Inspire them with the Holy Spirit to be people of zeal and mission, making Jesus known and loved near and far. Amen.'

The Priesthood

The Church continued to grow and spread across the ancient world despite some inhumane efforts on the part of Roman emperors to extinguish this new movement called Christianity. This new growth was welcomed but it put further strain on the ministry of the bishops in teaching, preaching and sanctifying the people of God. It is very difficult to pinpoint exactly when the following development took place but we know for sure that it did. A group began to emerge called *'presbyters'* who shared in the apostolic work of preaching the Gospel, teaching the faith and calling God's people to holiness.

In this sense, the emergence of the priesthood took place as a response to a growing need within the Church itself. As Catholics and Christians, we believe that this development was by the will of God and that the priesthood was and is his gift to his Church. We acknowledge that it was not something that came into existence suddenly or without the participation of the Christian community. The priesthood is one example of numerous developments that took place because God wanted them but that emerged within the social and cultural situation of the time. This further emphasises the point that God's spirit is always at work within the community and in the history of the world.

The bishops and the priests who minister in the Lord's name are servants of the communion of the Church. They are called to dedicate their lives to gathering all people and things into a unity with one another and with God. Bishops and priests in the Church work to ensure that all the gifts of the Spirit are ordered to flourish in harmony so that the life of the community may be enhanced. This work of 'ordering' gifts is far more than a practical way of preventing chaos. We believe that it is Christ's way of making the love of God visible to the world.

In these days when any institution of human authority is treated with suspicion, it is not uncommon to hear questions asked about the need for a Church hierarchy, and how it functions. We, as Catholics, believe that the hierarchy of the Church is there by divine origin, that its ministry is authenticated by the call to serve the communion of the Church worldwide and that it has come down to us from the apostles. However, we must always be mindful that the outward structures of the Church are mere skeletons if they do not serve the people of the Church and their life in the Spirit.

This call to serve the life in the Spirit is a noble and yet fragile one. The priest lives as a Christian among many and yet is called to something different: not better or worse, but different. He relies on the support of those entrusted to his care and yet is called to serve them with love and commitment. He struggles to preach God's word, addressing it first to himself as someone who has been touched by its power. He relies on the prayers of the community. He is carried by the community so that he is able in turn to sustain others by bringing them meaning and hope by the words he speaks of God.

Prayer:

*'Accept from the holy people of God the gifts to be
offered to him.
Know what you are doing and imitate the mystery
you celebrate:
Model your life on the mystery of the Lord's cross.
Amen.'*[2]

The Origins of the Papacy: St Peter

The ministry of the pope is founded on the role that St Peter had
in the college of apostles. There is strong evidence in the
Scriptures that Peter was appointed by Christ as the first among
the apostles. He was named by Christ as, 'The rock on which I
will build my Church' (Matthew 16:18ff). So too was he
commanded by Jesus to strengthen his brothers and sisters in the
faith, 'I have prayed for you Simon, that your faith may not fail,
and once you have recovered, you in your turn must strengthen
your brothers and sisters' (Luke 22:32). He was present with the
Lord for many of the significant moments of his life and, despite
his glaring weaknesses, he would go on to become a fearless
preacher of the Good News and a witness to Christ's love. Peter
was appointed by Jesus so that the apostles might be one and
undivided. When we bear in mind that the Gospels were written
some time after the Lord's resurrection, it suggests that Peter had
already begun to assume a role of leadership in the whole
Church and had become a figure of authority in regard to the
teaching of the faith and how it was to be understood (cf. Acts
15:7ff). He began to be seen as a figure of unity and communion
that he shared with the other apostles as their leader.

---

2   From the Rite of Ordination of a Priest.

Prayer:

'Lord Jesus, like Peter, I too try to follow you. Like Peter, I too try and fail. Help me to pray those beautiful words with him, "Lord, you know everything, you know that I love you". Amen.'

The Role of the Pope

As the years went by and as other men were appointed as successors to the apostles, so too did the Christian community appoint a successor to Peter. Thereafter the office of the Papacy was born. Catholics see in the Pope a visible sign of the unity of the Church. Through what he does and what he stands for, he calls all Christians to be united and personifies that same gift of unity that God has given the Church and the world.

As I write these words, the memories of the death and funeral of Pope John Paul II are still fresh in our minds. Who will forget those days of sadness and yet joy as we saw the fruit of the Pope's labours so evident in the people he united in life and in death? All his life, and especially since he became Pope, John Paul had dedicated himself to the work of reaching out to countries and other religions in order to further the cause of peace and reconciliation. At his funeral Mass in St Peter's Square, we caught a glimpse of how much he had achieved or rather how much God had achieved through him. At the largest funeral in living memory were gathered heads of State from countries all over the world, seated together in St Peter's Square and united in mourning on that April morning in 2005. Many of them represented countries that enjoyed good relations with the Pope but not with each other. Yet here they were together in the same space, united in mutual admiration and respect for the same man in whose honour they had come. If only for a few hours, we caught a glimpse of the dream for which Jesus had lived, suffered and died, 'May they all be one, just as Father, you are in me and I am in you' (John 17:21). Through his servant John Paul, God stirred up in us again the hope of unity and peace, not just in the Church but across the face of the earth.

Our understanding of the Church is real, visible and human. This we understand while still believing in its divine nature. We do not understand ourselves as a community that merely represents Christ in the world. Jesus was and is 'The Word who was made flesh and who dwelt among us' (John 1:14). He was the presence of the Father in human form, someone 'Who we have heard, who we have seen with our eyes, watched and touched with our hands' (1 John 1:1ff). In the same way we as the Church *are* his presence; his flesh and blood, his voice, his hands and feet. Even though God is not limited to his Church and remains God, the Church is still, 'The people whom God has taken as his own, for the praise of his glory' (Ephesians 1:14). As its centre of unity, the Pope represents this visible element of the Church and nourishes the faith of her members.

I recall a summer experience as a seminarian in South Bend, Indiana. One of the things that struck me forcibly was the number of Christian denominations that existed there. Driving around the city and countryside took me past several Churches, mostly with different names: there were the first Baptists; the Pentecostals, the Unitarian Church, the true Church of Christ, the Episcopalian Church, the Lutheran Church, the Methodist Church, the Catholic Church and so on.

It seemed good that so many Christian Churches existed but rather sad that there seemed to be a lack of cohesion between them, each having a different interpretation of the faith. When this is the case, the unity of the Church suffers and the effectiveness of her witness to the Gospel is reduced. The experience confirmed the Catholic belief that the Papacy is willed by God as an office to ensure communion between all the members of the Church around the world.

For many people today, the Catholic Church stands or falls on the Papacy. Some point to the scandals of the past and abuses of power as evidence of the Papacy being a human construction rather than a divine one. Yes, in the history of the Church there have been successors to this great office who have sanctioned deeds in the name of the Church and of God that were sinful and immoral. This point was acknowledged by Pope John Paul II himself in the Jubilee Year of 2000 when he publicly asked forgiveness for those sins of the past. Yet the fact that the Church still exists and has survived is testimony in itself of her origins in the mind of the Lord and as a great sign of God's power working through human weakness. When we recognise this in the facts of history we are not celebrating anything we have done, but praising the Lord who never abandons his Church.

Prayer:

'Loving God, you have called us to be part of your family, the Church.
May I love her as my own family. May I love her in her failings and in her strengths and may my life contribute something, however small, to the abundance of life she possesses. Amen.'

'I Believe in the Communion of Saints'

'A Holy Communion'

Central to our faith in the communion of saints is the theology of communion. It stretches our concept of the Church beyond the earthly horizon to include that of the world to come. We remind ourselves that the word 'communion' comes from the Greek word 'koinonia' which was the word used to describe the living relationship that God has called us to enjoy with him in Christ and the new way that this effected our relationships with one another. In other words, our communion has both vertical and horizontal dimensions, like the Lord's cross that symbolises it. Through him, in the Spirit, we are called into communion with God who wishes us to share his life. It is a communion of friendship, love, peace, forgiveness and a promise of the possibility to enjoy the company of God forever. This communion describes a living relationship with God that is so strong that it has no end. Not even death will destroy it. Through Jesus, God has promised us that he will never abandon us and that nothing on earth can ever separate us from the love of God made visible in Christ Jesus (cf. Romans 8:39). The only thing that can break this precious communion with God is human freedom. We remember that God can do all things bar one: force a human being to love him in return. Only if we walk away from the life that he is offering or live in a spirit that is contrary to the life of God can this communion with him be broken. We can walk away but God never will, for he cannot disown his own self.

However, if we remain in communion or relationship with God, we will inherit all he has promised in this life and in the next. Our communion with God brings us into the same communion with our neighbour and fellow Christian. Because of our communion with God through the same Jesus and in the same spirit, we share something very precious that is worth celebrating. Our common faith in the Lord brings us into closer contact and relationship. In the family of the Church we support and care for one another as we make our journey through life. We are part of the one family. We are brothers and sisters in Christ. Despite our diverse backgrounds we are bonded together like the early Church in Jerusalem whose life revolved around their faithfulness to the teaching of the apostles, to the Eucharist, to prayer and to their shared life in Christ (cf. Acts 2:42). In fact the Eucharist from the very beginning has been a celebration of that communion that we share. At the Mass we receive communion because we are in communion, with one another and with the Lord. Like our communion with Our Father through Jesus in the Spirit, so strong is our communion with each other that it is built to last forever. Nothing, not even death, is strong enough to break it.

Prayer:

'Grant that we, who are nourished by his body and blood,
may be filled with his Holy Spirit and become one
body, one spirit in Christ. Amen.'[1]

---

1   Eucharistic Prayer III.

Together Forever

What the communion of saints means for us who have lost husbands, wives, children, partners, relatives and friends is that even though they have gone from our sight, they are still in communion with us. They are in communion with God and they are in communion with us. If we believe that our loved ones who have died are with God and that God is everywhere then we also believe that they are everywhere, especially with those whose company they loved here on earth. St John Chrysostom once wrote something beautiful: 'our loved ones are no longer where they were before; they are now wherever we are'. By the fireside, at home in the kitchen where they were, there they still are. Out in the fields by the stream where they walked, there they still are. Wherever, whenever we remember them, pray for them, there they are. Wherever, whenever we praise God or come before him, there they are too. Whenever I live in my life the values that they inspired in me, there is their spirit.

As this theology suggests, the communion of saints is composed of thousands of millions of people who have lived on earth in communion with God and whose lives continue with him in the world to come. When our turn comes to pass through the gates of death, we will recognise the loved ones who have gone before us, professing their faith in God's love. We will embrace them in a way that will bring great joy and emotion, a moment that we have been longing for since they left us in body, but not in spirit. At that great moment we will recognise them as having been with us all along, albeit in a different way. There will be no need to explain the tears that we have shed for them, our loneliness, our pain, for they will have known it. They still walk with us along the road towards God and help prepare us for that day when we too will be called home by him. In this way our weakness is greatly helped by their concern (cf. 1 Timothy 2:5). As he was dying, St Dominic said to his brothers who surrounded him, 'Do not weep for I shall be more useful to you after my death and I shall help you then more effectively than during my life'. As the dead help us so we too can help them by our prayers, our sacrifices and our continued love that we bear towards them.

The theology of the communion of the saints is the basis of the Church's tradition of devotion to the saints. We all have our favourites for a variety of reasons. Many of them appeal to us because of their humanity, their struggle or because we recognise something of our own life in theirs. Perhaps we bear the name of our favourite saint. Whatever the reason, having devotion to a particular saint is very similar to having a soul friend or constant companion who now dwells in heaven and intercedes for us before God. Like the rest of our brothers and sisters in the Lord, we look forward to spending eternity in their company. We in the Church are part of a communion of charity that will last forever, 'For if we continue to love one another and join in praising the Most Holy Trinity, all of us who are children of God and form one family in Christ, we will be faithful to the deepest vocation of the Church'.[2]

Prayer:

'God Our Father, source of all holiness,
the work of your hands is manifest in your saints,
the beauty of your truth is reflected in their faith.
May we who aspire to have part in their joy
Be filled with the Spirit that blessed their lives,
So that having shared their faith on earth

---

2   *Lumen Gentium*, Vatican II.

We may also know their peace in your kingdom.
Grant this through Christ Our Lord. Amen.[3]

Conclusion

In summary, the communion of saints is a communion of love, friendship and companionship that we enjoy by virtue of our common faith in the Lord Jesus. This great communion includes the living and the dead, those in heaven, in purgatory and here on earth. This family of friendship in God is the place where we feel respected, cared for and where we belong. Among fellow Christians our need for moral companionship is nurtured and we feel supported in living the life of the Gospel. All of this offers hope and good news to so many. Individualism can leave us feeling isolated in our deepest beliefs and disconnected from those around us. We can have everything we want and be in need of nothing except what we desire most, namely this feeling of being supported by true friends. It is rightly said that as children we were dependent on others to survive, that as adolescents we fought to be independent but as adults we learn to be interdependent of each other. The Church is called to be a family that helps us to make these changes as we grow in life together. Church communities are called to foster lasting friendships that see another person as made in the image and likeness of God. We all need friendships. We can have hundreds of acquaintances and few friends. Despite the rapid advance in the means of communication, many today are very much alone, lonely, sometimes forced to look outside their own families and circles for the companionship and support for which they crave. With our belief in the communion of saints, the one who believes is

---

3   Opening Prayer: Feast of All Saints, 1 November.

never alone. Even in death, we are supported and strengthened by the Church on earth. In heaven, the saints are waiting to welcome us home. For all of us the communion of saints is a sign of hope and an invitation of faith to come and discover the wonderful life that God intends for us.

Prayer:

'Father All Powerful and ever living God,
we do well always and everywhere to give you thanks.
Around your throne the saints, our brothers and sisters,
Sing your praise forever.
Their glory fills us with joy, and their communion with us in your Church gives us inspiration and strength
As we hasten on our pilgrimage of faith, eager to meet them.
With their great company and all the angels we praise your glory as we cry out with one voice.'[4]

---

4 From Preface of Mass of All Saints, 1 November.

'I BELIEVE IN THE FORGIVENESS OF SINS'

Introduction

This article of faith in the Creed is made up of two parts. It focuses on the forgiveness of God and the reality of sin. In order for us to fully appreciate the love with which God has saved us, it is good to reflect first on what we have been saved from because 'It is the one who has been forgiven little who shows little love' (Luke 7:47).

The Reality of Sin

There was nothing pretty about Jesus' death on the cross. It was the most gruesome and humiliating death imaginable. Crucifixion forced a man to plummet the depths of suffering in a way that no one had ever done before. The victim of crucifixion was dehumanised in every possible way.

The prophet Isaiah reminds us in the liturgy on Good Friday that, 'Ours were the sufferings he was bearing, ours the sorrows he was carrying, while we thought of him as someone being punished and struck with affliction by God' (53:4). In the New Testament, Peter asks us to be always mindful of the price that Jesus paid in order to save us, 'What was the ransom that freed you? You know well enough that it was not paid with earthly currency, silver or gold; it was paid in the precious blood of Christ; no lamb was ever so pure, so spotless a victim' (1 Peter 1:17-19). On the cross, Jesus bore the full weight of humanity's sin. Out of love, he plummeted the depths of suffering and darkness in order to offer hope and forgiveness to all who wished to receive it. Sin is not only offensive to God but dehumanises humanity. The more we sin, the more we drift from God's love and the more we enter into a world of darkness, selfishness and corruption. Where there is an absence of God there are unspeakable deeds committed leading to despair and hopelessness. There is evil. There is hell.

On the cross and with his passion, Jesus absorbed all the guilt and sin of the human family on to himself. His cross shows us the horrific effects of sin and how much we should despise it. But Jesus, in the love that he bore towards us, willingly suffered and died for us so that we might be saved from the effects of sin, be forgiven and find a way back to God.

The horror of sin that caused his death was powerful. But the grace and the love of God was even greater. As St Paul reminds us, 'However much sin increased, grace was always greater' (Romans 5:20). God's love as revealed in Jesus was so strong that it could overcome the greatest evil and crime ever committed: the murder of love itself. We live in a beautiful and sad world. Every day, countless small and heroic acts of charity are silently carried out around the world by Christians and people of goodwill. Side by side is the existence of sin and its devastating consequences. Every news bulletin is evidence of that, for almost daily we hear another example of man's inhumanity to man.

As Christians, we must never tolerate sin. It is there in all our hearts. It is there among us as a community. Nor must we ever relativise sin. All sin is bad. When we choose to sin, we are choosing to settle for something less than God. We are choosing to sell ourselves short and to allow ourselves to become less human, throwing away the dignity that God bestowed upon us at such a high price.

Prayer:

'Almighty and Eternal God, you have restored us to life by the triumphant death and resurrection of Christ. Continue this healing work within us. May we who participate in this mystery never cease to serve you. We ask this through Christ Our Lord. Amen.'[1]

Repentance, Conversion and Renewal

Christians are called to be a people in touch with their own goodness given by God. After all, the Lord described us as 'The light of the world and the salt of the earth' (Matthew 5:13ff). However, as the Scriptures and human experience remind us, it is not the full picture. When we take an honest and hard look at ourselves, we recognise light and shadow, and our motives are not always pure. We are humbled when faced with the reality of our own sinfulness, our need for forgiveness and conversion. It is a call to see ourselves transparently before God: good and evil co-existing side by side in our hearts, in our lives and in the world. The Christian people believe that it is only Jesus Christ and his grace present to us that can enable us to maximise the good we have to offer but also to keep in check our potential for sin. If and when we sin, we believe that the gift of his forgiveness is freely available to us when we seek it.

The late Cardinal Hume once described the Church as a hospital for sinners rather than a club for saints. If ever there was a time for us as a Church to realise this, it is now. We who are part of the Church are a people who have come to know the

---

1   Closing Prayer: Service of Good Friday.

redeeming love of God in our own lives and who wish to proclaim its availability to all who believe. Recent years have seen a number of scandals exposed in many areas of political and Church life. The truth that tribunals and inquiries has revealed has led to the urgent task of shaping the future in a way that restores public confidence and leads to reform. The same applies to us as Church. But it would be wrong if our sole motivation for this elevation in moral standards were that of reclaiming our place in society or to be seen to do the right thing. Our first loyalty must be to the Word of God that calls us to 'Repent and believe in the Gospel' (Mark 1:15).

We must resist the temptation to construct Christianity without Christ. We must never gather in a room where he is not present, for if we do this, we lose our right to call ourselves Christians. If this happens we may well end up asking Christ to conform to our standards instead of conforming to his. At this time of uncertainty for the Church we must do our best to listen to the Lord and to become servants of his word in action. That gentle but firm voice calls us away from mindsets and ways of behaving that lead to nothing but unhappiness. There will always be failures, for, despite our spirits being willing to do good, our flesh is weak (cf. Mark 14:38). Nevertheless, the love of Christ tells us that we must never accept sin as being part of humanity. We remember from Calvary that sin dehumanises. A true humanity only comes without sin.

May we never lose sight of what God has called us to be in Christ, for 'He chose us in Christ before the world was made to be holy and faultless before him in love' (Ephesians 1:4). Sometimes we might feel that God is stretching us beyond our limits, but in faith we believe that he will never allow us to undergo anything that he will not give us the strength to endure. He invites us to remain close to him and not be afraid to ask for help when we feel that there is a pattern of behaviour in our lives that is becoming destructive. Jesus, who died for all, desires that in his Church the gates of forgiveness should always be open to anyone who turns away from sin. There is no offence, however serious, that Jesus cannot forgive, and the Church cannot forgive, in his name. Our God is a God of mercy, slow to anger and abounding in love. And so it is on this hopeful note that we turn our attention to the gift of God's infinite compassion.

Prayer:

'*O My God, I thank you for loving me. I am sorry for all my sins. For not loving others and not loving you, help me to live like Jesus and not to sin again. Amen.*'[2]

The Example of St Peter

The Church is held together on the gift of God's forgiveness. Without it she would cease to exist. The leadership of the Church exists today because of the unfailing gift of the Lord's mercy. Peter failed his Master in the worst possible way when he denied him three times. Yet the forgiveness of Jesus was his hope, for despite Peter's sin, it did not alter the plans the Lord had for him: 'I have prayed for you Simon, that your faith may not fail, and once you have recovered, you in your turn must strengthen your brothers' (Luke 22:31). Even more importantly, the Lord did not love him less because he had failed him. Jesus knew Peter and loved him as he was. He knew his strengths and his weaknesses too. He predicted his fall from grace and was forever trying to

---

2   Act of Contrition, Sacrament of Penance.

teach Peter the ways of God as opposed to the ways of humanity. Peter had to learn the hard way what it meant to be a disciple of the Lord. It happened only when Peter's face was covered in dust from the rubble of his own failures. At a meal the disciples shared with the risen Lord by the lake of Tiberias, Jesus singled out Peter and gave him the chance to reaffirm his love, having denied it three times. The positive response to the question, 'Simon, son of John, do you love me' (cf. John 21) was followed by the command of leadership and service to go and 'feed my sheep'. Despite Peter's failure, Jesus believed in him and reassured him of his love.

After his recovery and the coming of the Holy Spirit, Peter was a changed man. The Lord had forgiven him unconditionally and set him free from the imprisonment of his own sins and guilt. Peter's message to the Church was a proclamation of how the gift of God's mercy was available to all who asked for it in faith. To us he continues to say, 'I have neither silver nor gold but I will give you what I have: in the name of Jesus Christ the Nazarene, walk!' (Acts 3:6). Peter dedicated the rest of his life to proclaiming the forgiveness of sin in Jesus' name. It was a forgiveness that was unconditional and life changing. It remains a gift that is still offered to us today.

Prayer:

'Lord Jesus, you choose St Peter to be leader of your Church and strengthened him with your forgiveness and Spirit. May we, like him, never cease to proclaim you as our Saviour, brother and everlasting friend. Amen.'

The Gift of Forgiveness

The mercy of God is such that when we ask God to forgive us our sins, he does so in a way that restores our original innocence. From that moment, as far as God is concerned, our sin is forgiven and forgotten. As in the case of Peter, it will never be held against us. God does not love us less. A forgiveness that forgives but does not forget is not forgiveness at all. We as humans struggle to understand this reckless nature of God's mercy. We do so because our natural instincts are quite different. If we have a friend who wrongs us and who comes seeking our forgiveness, we may, depending on the betrayal, find it in our hearts to forgive them. But we rarely forget. We keep the incident at the back of our minds and our natural instincts warn us not to put ourselves in the position to be hurt again. This is very understandable because a sacred trust has been broken. We are very reluctant to take a chance on trusting them again.

Not so with God. He leaves himself open to be betrayed again and again out of the love that he bears towards us. Once he forgives us, he also forgets. We struggle to understand this or to accept the good news that it is. Instead we think that surely God will remember all the bad things we have done during our lives and throw them at us on the day of our judgement. We think that when we fail, God will give up on us, withdraw from us, believe in us less. We must be careful not to project on to God what we would do. It is only the revealed truth of Jesus Christ that tells us what God is truly like and it is the example of his life that teaches us the richness of his forgiveness. As in Peter's case, the Lord never holds our sins against us. Instead he draws closer to us, comes to look for us and rejoices when he finds us (cf. Luke 15:4-7; The Lost Sheep). The good shepherd's joy is to set us free and to grant us the gifts of healing and hope that come with his mercy. In Jesus we see the fulfilment of what is said of God in the psalms, 'If you O Lord should mark our guilt, Lord who would survive. But with you is found forgiveness, for this we revere you' (Psalm 129).

We believe that Jesus also willed that there be a horizontal dimension to attaining the gift of his forgiveness. Every sin has social consequences as does its opposite, love. It is more than a private matter between ourselves and God. Others are involved. If we love, others benefit. If we sin, others suffer. For this reason, Jesus conferred on his apostles his own divine power to forgive the sins of the community in his name, 'Receive the Holy Spirit. If you forgive the sins of any, they are forgiven; if you retain the sins of any, they are retained' (John 20:22-23). Therefore, when we come to celebrate the sacrament of penance, the priest present not only represents God at that moment but he also represents the community whose life has been damaged by our sins. In the name of God and in the name of the community, he ministers absolution. The gift of God's infinite mercy is the hope of all of us. It is our hope now and at the end of our lives. As one who knew the mercy of God, St Augustine reminds us that 'Were there no forgiveness of sins in the Church, there would be no hope of life to come or eternal liberation. Let us thank God who has given his Church such a gift'.[3]

Prayer:

'Lord Jesus Christ, your loving forgiveness knows no limits.
You took our human nature to give us an example of humility

---

3   *Sermons* 213, 8.

And to make us faithful in every trial.
May we never lose the gifts you have given us,
But if we fall into sin lift us up by your gift of
repentance,
You who live and reign forever and ever. Amen.[4]

---

4   From the Rite of Penance.

'I BELIEVE IN THE RESURRECTION OF THE BODY'

Rethinking Resurrection

Christian faith in the resurrection has often been met with incomprehension and opposition. Even more disputed is the belief in the resurrection of the body. It is commonly accepted in faith that the life of a human person continues in a spiritual fashion after death. But how can we believe that this body, so clearly mortal, could ever rise to everlasting life. Even practical evidence seems to contradict it.

Some of us may have been brought up with the strong belief that our souls are more important than our bodies, for it is our souls that live forever. Looking after our souls was far more important than looking after our bodies, for our bodies would one day die, releasing our souls for eternal life. Hence we thought that doing things like smoking, eating and drinking excessively and neglecting our health were independent of our relationship with God. We may have had a negative attitude towards our bodies, which saw our bodies as leading us into sin. Here was a spirituality that involved trying hard to discipline our bodies in order to reach unity with God. Intimacy with God came by bypassing our bodily needs rather than finding God through them. Does our faith in the resurrection of the body support or challenge these assumptions?

Our belief that our bodies will rise again on the last day is based on our faith in the resurrection of Jesus Christ. Earlier, in the chapter on the resurrection, we saw some of the implications of Jesus' life continuing in a glorious way after his death on the cross. He was raised to life by the Father on the third day and revealed himself to those who were closest to him. From the Gospel passages that outline some of his appearances after his resurrection, two aspects stand out. The first is that he was in some way different than before when they did not recognise him (cf. Luke 24:16). He had the power to pass through closed doors (cf. John 20:19).

The second aspect of the risen Christ that we notice from the Gospel texts was that even though the risen Jesus was in some way different than before, he was still the same person they had known before his death. He was the same Jesus of Nazareth who had travelled with them, ate with them for the previous three years and whom they had watched die on Calvary. Jesus' body had been transformed but he still bore the wounds of the cross (cf. Luke 24:40) on his glorified body. To emphasise the material aspect of his glorified body he even took a piece of grilled fish 'which he ate before their eyes' (Luke 24:42). So also did he invite Thomas to place his hands in his wounds to show that his risen presence was something very real and yet connected with how they knew him before (cf. John 20:27-29). The bodily aspect to the Lord's resurrection is further emphasised by the Gospel accounts of the empty tomb (cf. Matthew 28:1-8; Mark 16:1-8; Luke 24:1-11; John 20:1-18). It was not as if Jesus had his old body replaced by a new one. Somehow, by God's power, Jesus' body that had been battered and broken on the cross had been transformed in a new and wonderful way. The whole person of Jesus was transformed by the resurrection: body and soul. The resurrection of the Lord was both bodily and spiritual all at once.

When we come to consider our faith in the resurrection of the body, we do so in the light of the resurrection of Jesus. The resurrection of the Lord is the foundation stone not only of this article of faith but of faith as a whole. Our faith stands or falls on it. As St Paul reminds us, 'How can some of you say that there is no resurrection of the dead? But if there is no resurrection of the dead, then Christ has not been raised; if Christ has not been raised, then our preaching is in vain and your faith is in vain ... But in fact Christ has been raised from the dead, the first fruits of those who have fallen asleep' (1 Corinthians 15:12-14, 20). The bodily and spiritual transformation that happened to Jesus at the resurrection, we believe will happen to us on the last day. This we believe through faith. Our resurrection will be the work of the Most Holy Trinity: 'If the Spirit of him who raised Jesus from the dead dwells in you, he who raised Christ Jesus from the dead will give life to your mortal bodies also through his spirit who dwells in you' (Romans 8:11). The Spirit of God that we possess is the same powerful spirit that raised Jesus from the dead. We possess a transforming power within us that bestows the fruits of the resurrection on this side of the grave as well as in the life to come and on the last day. We do not have to wait until we are dead to experience something of the glory that awaits us in the next life. The power of transformation that comes with faith in the resurrection is brought to bear here and now in this life and will be fulfilled in the world to come.

When we believe in the resurrection of Jesus, its transforming power occurs immediately in the life of the believer. It makes all things new. It transforms and unites us as people and as communities. No longer does there exist a split between body and soul as if one mattered more than the other. Both were created by God and were taken and redeemed by Jesus Christ. With our share in Jesus' bodily resurrection, both are changed and we become more like him. With the resurrection of Jesus, God has taken up residence in our humanity and from there transforms it from within, for 'The

Word was made flesh and dwelt among us' (John 1:14). No aspect of our humanity has been left untouched by the Spirit of the risen Christ. If we acknowledge this then we realise that Christian faith calls us to have a more positive approach to our bodies, our health and our general well being because these too are very precious in the eyes of God. We do not have the right to do with our bodies whatever we like because ultimately we are their stewards, not their owners. Our bodies are gifts from God and they deserve our care. They are sacred because the body of a Christian is the temple of the Holy Spirit; 'The body is meant for the Lord and the Lord for the body. The God who raised the Lord Jesus will also raise us up by his power. Do you not know that your bodies are members of Christ? ... You are not your own ... So glorify God in your body' (1 Corinthians 6:13-15; 19-20). This truth is even further pressed home when we celebrate the Eucharist and receive the Body and Blood of the Lord. When this happens, his own flesh and blood is absorbed into ours.

Over the centuries, some of the fiercest critics of Christianity have objected that it focused too much on suffering, death and the next life, effectively destroying our capacity to enjoy this one. This criticism contains some truth to the extent that we used to think of the resurrection as something that was only relevant after death. The full extent to which we already share in the resurrection remains a mystery because, as the Scriptures teach us, our lives 'remain hidden with Christ in God' (Colossians 3:3). Yet we believe that with the gift of faith, the Father has already 'Raised us up with him and made us sit with him in the heavenly places in Christ Jesus' (Ephesians 2:6). Hence faith in the resurrection has to do with this life *and* the world to come when we will share fully what we already share partly now. Let us look closer at the effects of this transforming power in three parts: sharing in the resurrection now, sharing in the resurrection after death and sharing in the resurrection on the last day.

Prayer:

'Loving God, because you raised Jesus to life, we believe that love can never die. May the power of the resurrection possess my life, my body, my soul. May it lead me forward until that day when I will share fully in the life you have already begun in me. Amen.'

Sharing in the Resurrection Now

Faith in the Lord's resurrection affects a change in who we are, body and soul. As we grow older, we mature, realising over time that many sacrifices need to be made if our lives are to bear fruit. We become aware that we cannot experience everything. The tensions, frustrations and unfulfilled dreams that we hold in our lives can be transformed by God's grace into many other gifts we receive in life and maybe hadn't expected to. Life teaches us to let go, to die to ourselves, to give freely in order to receive back even more. This paradox was summed up by Jesus himself when he taught us that 'Unless a wheat grain falls to the earth and dies, it remains but a single grain, but if it dies, it yields a rich harvest. Anyone who loves their life will lose it and anyone who hates their life will keep it for eternal life' (John 12:24-25). It is only in giving to the world that we receive, it is in forgiving that we are forgiven and it is in dying that we are born to eternal life. Seeing life this way comes about only by God's grace and with our faith in the Lord's resurrection. Only by being close to Jesus can we ever hope to be like him. We need the gift of faith to see how our losses are compensated by new life that comes in different ways.

Here lies the challenge. As we get older, we are all well aware that even if we are advancing in the spiritual life, our bodies seem to be going in the opposite direction. The wear and tear of the years seem to bring more visits to the doctor, less hair, more wrinkles and a realisation that life indeed is very short. The effect that the years have on our bodies challenges us as to where our securities lie. Growing old can be very difficult to accept, especially if it forces us to let go of something or someone that gave us pride and security when we were younger. For many of us, ageing can bring with it a host of issues around the meaning and direction of our lives and our acceptance by others. These feelings are very real and they are complex. At first glance it can seem as if there are many losses and few obvious gains. But gain we do. We who suffer losses ultimately become stronger and more mature, provided we are open to the gift of faith and the Spirit of God. The fruits of the resurrection might be a little obscure, but they are there. Here are some examples of what we may lose in life and gain as our journey progresses:

- In middle age we may lose some of our youthful looks but realise that what's inside is just as important as how we look on the outside.
- In retirement we may lose income, but we find more freedom to do the things maybe we had no time for before.
- In old age we may lose a little independence, but we receive back some of the love we gave to others.
- Often when we lose possessions in life, we find after mourning their loss we are freer and less burdened, realising that we were meant to travel lightly through this world.
- Sometimes when relationships end, we learn who we are – not in relation to other people, but just as ourselves.
- We may lose items or abilities, only to realise how much we appreciate that which we have left.

From a faith perspective, these are experiences that challenge us to deepen our trust in God's eternal love for us. Getting older and edging closer to death can make us feel terrified or can be seen as God's way of drawing us closer to himself and to the place we are destined to be for all eternity. Realising this can bring a wonderful peace and acceptance. We are constantly dying to one type of reality and rising to another. In the words of St Paul to the Corinthians, 'Even though our physical being is gradually decaying, yet our spiritual being is renewed day after day' (2 Corinthians 4:16). As we weaken in one way, we are made stronger in another. The truth of Christ's dying and rising is not a message of the Church that echoes into an empty space because dying and rising to new life is something that is part of daily living. We tend to associate death and resurrection only with physical death and what comes afterwards but these things will make sense only when we see how they are connected to the rhythm of life that is going on all the time. It is a law that is written into nature. Autumn and winter bring death, spring and summer burst into life and colour. So too with humanity. We change, we grow, we think and act differently than we used to. Each day can make a difference. St Augustine, for example, used to refer to sleep as a 'daily death'[1] because part of us dies with every day that passes. However, it can also be said that every time we wake up and welcome a new day, we share again in the resurrection, for a new path opens out before us that offers us many new opportunities to love, to learn and to achieve our potential.

St Paul developed the point further when he spoke of the fruitfulness of the cross and that when we are in Christ, death and loss are always followed by resurrection and new life. In his letter to the Philippians he describes all things as loss 'Because

---

1   *Letter* 151 to *Caecilian.*

of the supreme advantage of knowing Christ Jesus my Lord'
(3:8). All Paul prays for is that he 'May come to know him and
the power of his resurrection, partake in his sufferings by being
moulded into the pattern of his death, striving towards the goal
of resurrection' (3:10-11). We too proclaim the same faith at the
Eucharist, when we say, 'Lord by your cross *and* resurrection,
you have set us free. You are the saviour of the world'
(Acclamation of Faith). In other words, Jesus has saved us both
by his death and rising to new life, a gift that he shares
abundantly with all of us who believe.

Prayer:

> *'We therefore pray thee, Lord, that this candle*
> *hallowed in honour of thy name, may continue*
> *bravely burning to dispel the darkness of this night.*
> *Welcome it as a sweet fragrance, mingling with the*
> *lights of heaven. May the morning star find its flame*
> *alight, that morning star which knows no setting,*
> *which came back from the grave and shed its clear*
> *light upon humankind.*'[2]

Sharing in the Resurrection after Death

What the next life will be like exceeds our imagination and
understanding; it is accessible only by faith. At our baptism we
were inserted into the life, death and resurrection of Jesus. At
that moment God gave us his life and the fruits of his
resurrection. Provided we accept this gift of faith and live it
here on earth, God has promised us that we will see the light of

---

2   Pascal Proclamation.

his face once we die. We are encouraged to persevere in the Christian life by the words of Paul who wrote that 'No eye has seen, no ear has heard, things beyond the mind of man what God has prepared for those who love Him' (1 Corinthians 2:9). Cardinal Bernadin of Chicago wrote a book entitled *The Gift of Peace* and completed it only a few weeks before he died of cancer in 1996. In the book he wrote with remarkable courage about his own death:

> Many people have asked me what I think the next life will be like ... Of course I do not know for sure but something tells me that if and when I get there, I will have the feeling that I have been there before. Let me explain. My parents grew up and met in Italy before they emigrated to the United States. As a child, they told me wonderful stories about the place where they grew up. These stories filled me with excitement with the thoughts of one day going there to see for myself. When that day came, I stood on Italian soil, in thc village where my parents grew up and the powerful feeling came over me that I had been here before.[3]

In some way, perhaps, this is what awaits us when we die. We will have the feeling that we have been here before. Perhaps it will fully dawn on us then that we have just completed our pilgrimage on earth, our exile and that we are now finally home. This feeling will be further boosted by the welcome of loved ones gone before us but most of all by our God who has accompanied us on every step of life's journey. For eternity we will rejoice in the presence of God, caught up and immersed in

---

3   Joseph Cardinal Bernadin, *The Gift of Peace*, Chicago, Loyola Press, 1997.

his beauty, peace and love. There we shall experience fully what we have tasted in this life and marvel at the things God has prepared for those who love him.

Prayer:

> *'May he support us all the day long,*
> *till the shades lengthen and the evening comes,*
> *and the busy world is hushed,*
> *and the fever of life is over and our work is done!*
> *Then in his mercy may he give us a safe lodging and*
> *a holy rest*
> *And peace at last.*
> *Complete thy work, O Lord, and as you have loved*
> *me from the beginning so make me to love you unto*
> *the end. Amen.'*[4]

Sharing in the Resurrection on the Last Day

Jesus longs for us to be with him. He 'thirsts for us' (cf. John 19:28). He wants us to be where he is. He is the first to rise again in body and spirit. He has promised us that those who believe in him will also rise again and share fully in his resurrection. But we must wait for this to happen.

Yes, we already share in his resurrection as we have seen. But even after our death we are told there will be a period of waiting until the last day at the end of time. It will be the day that we have anticipated every time we have celebrated the Mass and proclaimed the acclamation of faith, 'Christ has died, Christ is risen, *Christ will come again'*. On that glorious day, all

---

4   Cardinal Newman.

the just will rise again with their own bodies, which will be transformed to be like the glorious body of Christ (cf. Philippians 3:21; 1 Corinthians 15:44). On that day, God will not only raise up our bodies, but the whole of his creation will be transformed into the image that God intended since the beginning. The 'new heaven and the new earth' will be complete (cf. Rev. 21:5) and God's dream will be fulfilled. It is the day we are waiting for until the Lord returns as he promised. This day is looked forward to with hope by all Christians who remain faithful. Then, in the presence of Christ, the truth of each person's relationship with God will be laid bare. The Last Judgement, as we call it, will reveal once and for all that God's justice triumphs over all the injustices committed by his creatures and that God's love is stronger than death and sin. On that day, finally, God will be 'All in all' (1 Corinthians 15:28).

We know not the moment when all of this will happen, for God alone has decided. What he asks of us is to be ready, prepared and waiting for the bridegroom to return (cf. Matthew 25:1-13). In the meantime, as we wait, our faith does not call us to remain idle. Far from diminishing our concern to develop the earth, the expectancy of a new earth should spur us on, for it is here that the body of a new human family grows, foreshadowing in some way the age which is to come. That is why, although we must be careful 'to distinguish earthly progress clearly from the increase of the kingdom of Christ, such progress is of vital concern to the kingdom of God, insofar as it can contribute to the better ordering of human society.'[5] Together we are called to become God's instruments in ushering in this new age and building a civilisation of love where 'God's will is done on earth as it is in heaven'.

---

5   *Gaudium et Spes*, Vatican II, 39.

Prayer:

'*Deliver us Lord from every evil and grant us peace in our day. In your mercy keep us free from sin and protect us from all anxiety as we wait in joyful hope for the coming of our Saviour, Jesus Christ.*'[6]

---

6   Communion Rite of the Mass.

'I BELIEVE IN LIFE EVERLASTING'

The Reality of Death

As we get older, life makes us more aware of the truth that, someday, we will die. When we pray the rosary we ask Mary fifty times to pray for us 'Now and at the hour of our death'. When this will be, none of us know. We all would like it to be in our own bed, surrounded by the people we love, but there is no guarantee of this and many times, as experience teaches us, death comes in a different way. We fear it because our natural instinct is to live. We have a powerful instinct to survive and do not want to surrender to death, which robs us of what we value most. The fear of death has always been there but perhaps never more than today.

One of the pressing religious questions that humanity has always asked itself is that of our destiny and calling. Where have we come from and where are we going? Does it all end when we die? Do I think about my own death? Do I prepare for it? As Christians, it is important for us to confront the reality of death honestly and to realise the great hope that our faith brings in the face of it. This the Church does in a special way during the month of November. It is the month 'set aside' for us to contemplate this mystery together. Doing so helps us to appreciate the gift of our lives that we enjoy now and to make the most of the opportunities that God has given us today.

Jesus Christ, the Son of God, himself suffered death that is part of the human condition. Yet, despite the anguish he suffered as he faced death, he accepted it as an act of submission to the will of the Father. It was his final act of abandonment to God and trust in the God he loved, 'Father, into your hands I commend my Spirit' (Luke 23:46).

Prayer:

'My brother/sister in faith,
I entrust you to God who created you.
May you return to the one who formed you from the
dust of this earth.
May Mary, the angels and the saints come to meet
you as you go forth from this life. May Christ who
was crucified for you bring you freedom and peace.
May Christ the Son of God who died for you take you
into his kingdom.
May Christ the Good Shepherd give you a place
within his flock.
May he forgive your sins and keep you among his
people. May you see your redeemer face to face and
enjoy the sight of God forever. Amen.'[1]

Life after Death

For the Christian, death is not the end. With the resurrection of Jesus, God transformed the meaning of death forever. Now, instead of it being the end, it is a new beginning. It is to be the beginning of a new life that continues in God's presence in another place and in another way. Death is like a second birth that we must undergo before we are born to the fullness of

---

1   From the Rite and Anointing and Care of the Sick and Dying.

eternal life. It is like a gateway that we must pass through on our way to life with God forever. As St Therese of Lisieux wrote before she died, 'I am not dying; I am entering life'. As Christians are asked to try to look at death with hope, knowing that the Lord Jesus has already won the victory over death on the cross. To contemplate our death may not be a pleasant thing to do but can be a very healthy spiritual exercise, because facing it with courage can remove any control it may have over us. St Francis of Assisi referred to death in friendly terms when he called it 'sister death'. In contemplating his own life and death, St Paul wrote, 'For me Christ is life and death is gain'. Such was the faith of Francis and Paul in the resurrection of Jesus that they were no longer afraid of death. With the resurrection of Jesus, it had lost its power. It is important for us to keep death in perspective and to always see it in connection to life. This means not only thinking about it as something that comes at the end of our journey but also as something that is with us all along through life. Many of us like to walk along the beach. Many of us find it a spiritual experience and an opportunity for refreshment as we walk along the interface between land and sea. As you walk along the shore, imagine for a moment that the land on your right side represents this life and the sea on your left side represents the next life. Already we begin to appreciate something more of what it means to believe in the communion of saints. We begin to realise that the dividing line between the two worlds is but a short distance. We realise that the world beyond us does not only lie ahead of us in the future but is present beside us all the time. Just as the sea penetrates the land on the shore, so too does the next life spill into every moment of this one.

Every act of faith can be a time when we reach beyond ourselves and be intimately present to God and all the saints who come to meet us. With this way of looking at death, we see it as not only something that lies ahead but rather something that accompanies us always. Contemplating our own death can bring with it a good deal of fear. I have had the privilege of being with many people as they prepared for their own death. Many of them experience a natural fear of dying and even of meeting God face to face. I recall those times with gratitude to God for allowing me to be a messenger of hope and his love. Very often it would be an opportunity to recall the words of Jesus in the Gospel of John where he says, 'You did not choose me, no I choose you ... I no longer call you servants but friends' (John 15:15ff). It is a very consoling thought that at the moment of death we will be met not by a stranger but by a friend. Not just by an acquaintance but by a great friend; the greatest one we ever had. Jesus will come to meet us at the moment of death with his loving arms extended to embrace us in a wonderful moment of intimacy, forgiveness and love. To those who have done his will on earth, he will then whisper those words that we all hope to hear, 'Come you blessed of my Father, take as your heritage the kingdom prepared for you since the foundation of the world' (Matthew 25:34). The fact that we don't know when this moment will be is also a good thing, for it creates in us a necessary urgency to live a good life in God, repent of our sins and be ready: 'See that you have your belts done up and your lamps lit. Be like people waiting for their master to return from the wedding feast, ready to open the door as soon as he comes and knocks. Blessed those servants whom the master finds awake when he comes' (Luke 12:35-37). We stand ready and hopeful. Our hope in the face of death comes from the bond of our relationship of love that we enjoy with Our Lord Jesus, 'For I am certain of this, neither death nor life ... will ever come between us and the love of God, known to us in Christ Jesus our Lord' (Romans 8:39). The power of this bond of love that we have with God will carry us over the threshold of death and into the next life where we will exist in one of two states: Purgatory or Heaven. In the next life, Scripture and the tradition of the Church tell us that only those who have willingly rejected the gift of communion with God in this life will exist in a state we refer to as 'Hell'.

Prayer:

'Father, all powerful and ever living God,
We do well always and everywhere to give you thanks
through Jesus Christ Our Lord.
In him who rose from the dead, our hope of
resurrection dawned.
The sadness of death gives way to the bright promise
of immortality.
Lord for your faithful people, life is changed, not
ended.
When the body of our earthly dwelling lies in death,
We gain an everlasting dwelling place in heaven.
And so with all the choirs of angels in heaven we
proclaim your glory
And join in their unending hymn of praise.'[2]

Heaven

Sharing God's Glory
All of us imagine from time to time what heaven will be like. None of us can know for sure, but we all hope to find out some day! Every image we use to describe it inevitably falls short of

---

2   First Preface from Mass for the Dead.

its reality because our minds and imagination are simply too limited to understand. St Paul predicts the wonderful experience it will be and imagines it to be way beyond anything we had possibly dreamed, 'What no eye has seen and no ear has heard, what the mind of humanity cannot visualise; all that God has prepared for those who love him' (1 Corinthians 2:8). Referring back to the story in the last chapter about Cardinal Bernadin, I suspect like he did, that somehow we may have the feeling that we have been there before. In other words, there are moments when the experience of heaven spills into our life experience on earth and prepares us for the joys of the life to come.

The glimpses we get of heaven, the foretaste of what is to come, are all too fleeting and temporary. Like Peter, James and John with the Lord on Mount Tabor at the Transfiguration, we all must come down from the mountain and live the ordinary that is everyday life (cf. Luke 9:28). Nevertheless, these precious times of joy and peace are a promise of the future glory that lies ahead for all those who remain faithful to God. The meaning of things and their purpose is now partly hidden but shall in the end become clear.

St Paul touches on this when he writes in his letter to the Corinthians, 'Now we see only reflections in a mirror, mere riddles, but then we shall be seeing face to face' (1 Corinthians 13:12).

The Lord Jesus speaks often to us about heaven in the Scriptures. To do this, he often uses images that best describe the experience of friendship with God that is beyond all understanding and description. Images are used of light, peace, life, a wedding feast, good wine, the Father's house, the heavenly Jerusalem and paradise. Those who share heaven will contemplate and adore God forever, for they will 'See him as he is, face to face' (1 John 3:2). There, with Mary, the angels and saints, they adore the Most Holy Trinity, Father, Son and Holy Spirit and never cease praying for the human family on earth. Heaven is the place or state where there is perfect fulfilment of our deepest human longings, where there is no more sorrow or suffering but supreme happiness in praising God forever. Our faith in God unites us to him eternally in the present moment. It is the 'Eternal Now'. In heaven we will also take part in the 'Eternal Wow!' of God where we will be absorbed in awe, wonder and admiration of the beauty and love of God that will consume us. There we will be with Christ whose life, death and resurrection has made all of it possible. If and when we reach heaven, with St Paul we suspect its joy will be beyond anything we could have dreamed of or conceived. When we enter its courts to be greeted by the loving arms of our God, all the suffering, trials and tribulations that we experienced in life will melt away into insignificance when compared with that moment, for 'All that we suffer in the present time is nothing in comparison with the glory which is destined to be disclosed for us' (Romans 8:18).

Prayer:

'May he make us an everlasting gift to you
and enable us to share in the inheritance of the
saints with Mary,
the Virgin mother of God;
with the apostles and martyrs and all the saints on
whose constant intercession we rely for help.'[3]

---

3   From Eucharistic Prayer III.

On our Way Home

Our faith calls us to view things from an eternal perspective. Life is very short. It is passing away and changing daily. We are on a pilgrimage here on earth that will not last forever. One day it will end and will then continue in a different way. Our faith tells us that God is preparing us all the time for the joy that lies in store. God is continually stretching us and expanding our horizons so that we might become more and more like Jesus his son and more the people he wants us to be. All along the journey of life, he is calling us, teaching us, blessing us, feeding us, forgiving us, healing us and, most importantly, loving us. All the time God is leading us on, leading us home. Even when he allows troubles to be part of what we endure, God has greater good in mind. Our troubles are often the tools by which God fashions us for better things. If and when we reach heaven, we will bask with joy in the presence of sheer and utter love, who is God himself. In one perfect and eternal moment, it will all make sense.

On the feast day of All Saints on 1 November each year we pause to celebrate the gift of God's grace and love that shine through those who enjoy the light of heaven. Counted among them are not only the canonised saints of the Church but all the people that we have known and loved in this life and who taught us something more about God's everlasting love and mercy. These were the people who shaped our lives and who helped us to become the people we are today. In life as in death, they reflect the light of God to us as the moon reflects the light of the sun. They live in God's presence, praying for us always and interceding with God on our behalf. Where they have gone we hope to follow at a time decided only by God.

On our part, we also are called to love them in return and not to forget their need for our support and companionship. 'Out of sight, out of mind' is a temptation for us when it comes to the dead, which is why the Church helps to direct our minds towards them especially in the month of November but also at times like patron days, anniversaries and birthdays.

Scripture tells us that, 'It is a good and wholesome thought to pray for the dead' (Maccabees 12:46). As fellow believers we can help those who are still on their pilgrim way to the fullness of life in heaven. That is, the holy souls in purgatory.

Prayer:

'Loving God, show me the place of green pastures and restful waters, lead me to the grass which nourishes, call me by name so that I who am your sheep may hear your voice. Give me by your voice eternal life. Speak to me, you whom my soul loves.'[4]

Purgatory

As a priest who has presided at funerals, I often found myself in a dilemma when preparing the homily. On one hand, the intention was there to offer as much support possible to the grieving family and to assure them that their loved ones were now with God and at peace. On the other hand, I sometimes felt that this was done at the expense of inviting the community to pray and to make sacrifices of love for all those who have died. The presumption seems to be there that the person who had died was already in heaven. In other words, the doctrine of purgatory gets lost in the middle.

---

4   St Gregory of Nyssa, *Commentary on the 'Song of Songs'*, Massachusetts: Hellenic College Publishing, 1987, Chapter 2.

It is certainly not the intention of anyone to upset people whose friends or family members have died. However, the challenge remains not to gloss over our faith in purgatory but rather to rediscover that it is the love of God and not fiery flames that will lead to our purification.

The best teaching on purgatory that I have read was by the late Cardinal Basil Hume in his book, *To Be A Pilgrim*.[5] There, the Cardinal reflected on the fifth chapter of St Luke's Gospel where Jesus' power was responsible for a miraculous catch of fish (cf. Luke 5:1ff). After the miracle, the Gospel tells us that Peter, on seeing what had happened, fell down at the knees of Jesus and said, 'Leave me Lord; for I am a sinful man!' (5:8). Luke tells us that all his companions were completely awestruck at the catch they made (cf. 5:8ff).

What was happening here? It seems that Peter, the leader of the apostles and symbolic head of the Church, was completely overcome by the glory of God that he saw before him. He now stood naked before the goodness and the mercy of God. He seemed blinded by the purity and brightness of God's glory before him. His first reaction was to fall on his knees and to say, 'Leave me Lord; for I am a sinful man!'. Peter was overwhelmed by a sense of his own inadequacy, sinfulness and human mortality when confronted by the glory of God that had come close to him. He was overcome by a sense of his own unworthiness and was willing to leave the Lord until he was more prepared to share in the beauty and glory that he experienced on that day.

Maybe, just maybe, this is what purgatory will be like. At the moment of our death we will be confronted by the glory of God as Peter was that day by the Lake of Gennesaret. Like him, we will willingly depart for a while to another place or state in order to prepare to contemplate the face of God in heaven.

---

5   London: Triangle Publications, 1988.

What this will be like, we simply do not know. Perhaps on one hand it will be painful to be absent from heaven but also joyful knowing that one day, the time will come when we will be welcomed there by God and the whole company of saints.

The Church gives the name 'purgatory' to this state or place of purification or cleansing. The holy souls in purgatory are still in communion with God, which is their source of greatest joy. So too are they in communion with us and look to us to help them and pray for them. The Church asks us in charity not to forget them but to offer alms, prayers and sacrifices of love on their behalf which support them on their way.

Prayer:

'O Most Holy Trinity, Father, Son and Holy Spirit,
I adore you profoundly,
And I offer up to you this day the sacred Body, Blood, Soul and
Divinity of Jesus Christ, in union with all the Masses celebrated throughout the world this day, for the holy souls in purgatory;
For sinners everywhere and sinners in my own home and family. Amen.'

'Eternal rest grant onto them O Lord and let perpetual light shine upon them.
May they rest in peace. Amen.'

Hell

Self-Exclusion
God loves us with an infinite love, but he has also given us free will and choice. Just as loving is an act of our freedom, so too is

sin. Since we have free will, it is possible for us to reject God. Since free will exists, hell also exists. Like heaven, Jesus discussed its reality. He portrayed it as a place of pain that comes from a human person being separated from God for all eternity (cf. Matthew 13:50; 25:31-46). The fear of hell terrifies people and raises the question as to how any loving God could send anyone to hell. The answer to this is that God never sends anyone to hell. The teaching of the Church is clear in this regard, for 'God wants all people to be saved and come to the knowledge of the truth' (1 Timothy 2:4). God does not wish that any of his children be apart from him. The Catechism does not say that anyone has ever gone to hell, only that it remains a possible human choice.

The human person is a free and responsible being. We decide whether to love and let ourselves be loved. While we say that we believe in hell as a possibility, we must not say for certain that there is anyone there. To do so would be to take the judgement of God into our own hands which we simply cannot do. Even the most evil people in the world's history have God as their judge and him alone.

This teaching of hell and the Church's proclamation of God's mercy are not on the same level, for God's 'yes' to us is always stronger than our 'no' to him: 'However much sin increased, grace was always greater' (Roman 5:20). Nevertheless the possibility of hell can and does remind us of the importance of conversion and repentance from sin in the life of every Christian. It is an invitation not to postpone our need for conversion until another day. It begins now and we must be ready and faithful. We know not the day nor the hour. We cannot fool God. We cannot say 'yes I believe' and then deliberately sin against him. Before God there is no hiding place for we are constantly exposed to his truth. In him, 'Everything now covered will be uncovered, and everything now hidden will be made clear' (Luke 12:2). Outward actions are reflections of interior dispositions. We cannot hope for eternal life if the fruits of goodness are not seen somewhere in our lives. This warning from the Lord himself, comes sharply into focus in relation to the poor (cf. Matt 25: 31ff). Through them, Christ presents himself to us and invites a response. One response is to ignore them; another is to come to their help. Both responses have consequences that St Matthew outlines clearly and that we are familiar with. In so far as we did anything to the least of his brothers and sisters, we did it to him.

It is God alone who knows the promptings of grace within someone's heart. If we look into our hearts we will discover how that voice is calling us to respond. For those who are not Christian and those without faith, God's offer of love and salvation is not denied to them. They too will be judged according to how they have responded to the grace of God in their hearts and lives as a whole. At the Eucharist we pray for all people of goodwill and 'all those who seek you with a sincere heart' (Eucharistic Prayer IV). We pray that every human being God has made will be gathered together in his life and love for all eternity. In that family of God we pray with Jesus that 'Not one is lost' (John 17:12).

Prayer:

'*O my Jesus,*
Forgive us our sins,
Save us from the fires of hell.
Lead all souls to heaven,
Especially those in most need of your mercy.'[6]

---

6   Prayer of the Rosary.

Confronting Evil

When we look around the world today few can deny the presence of evil. At the same time, we believe that Jesus has beaten sin and death with his life, death and resurrection. We share in his victory. We recall that in Jesus' life and ministry, he was confronted with the powers of darkness and evil that had to be overthrown to give way to the kingdom of heaven. Today, the Church is still grappling with this presence of evil and sin that tarnishes her members and that confronts her as she furthers the mission entrusted to her by the Lord himself. We only have to look at our recent history for continuing evidence of how evil scars the conscience of humanity: Auschwitz, Hiroshima, Cambodia, Oklahoma, 11 September, Rwanda and many more. The list goes on and on. We don't even have to look far from our own homes to hear of or experience the cruelties we inflict on one another. Even in our own country, there are daily reports of violence, abuses and injustices committed against our fellow human beings.

Like Jesus, we are involved in a battle with the powers of darkness that threaten to take us away from God and lead us to self-destruction. By remaining faithful to him, we know that this will not happen. With our lives in Christ, we believe that he has already shared his victory with us. However, we must never cease to pray and to confront evil wherever it is found. We must have the courage to carry the light of Christ to those places that are darkest: 'While you still have the light, believe in the light so that you may become children of the light' (John 12:36). In this task we are inspired by the example of Jesus himself who prayed to his Father on the night before he died, 'I am not asking you to remove them from the world but to protect them from the Evil One' (John 17:15). In the end, the reality is a simple one: if humanity lives in unity and peace with God its creator, it will prosper and know peace. If it chooses not to then we self-destruct. As Oscar Romero wrote from the darkness and violence of El Salvador, 'Without God, humans are wild beasts. Without God they are deserts. Their hearts have no blossoms of love. They are only the perverse persecutors of their brothers and sisters'.[7]

Oscar Romero is just one of the countless witnesses to God's victory over evil and whose words and example encourage us to remain faithful to the way of Jesus, the way of peace, truth and love. On our daily journey through life may the Lord 'lead us not into temptation but deliver us from evil'.

Prayer:

'Father of eternal life, you are a God, not of the dead but of the living:
you sent your Son to proclaim the good news of life,
to rescue men and women from the kingdom of death
and to lead them to resurrection.
Free these chosen people from the power of the evil spirit who brings death. May they receive new life from Christ and bear witness to his resurrection.
We ask this through Christ Our Lord. Amen.'[8]

---

7   *The Violence of Love*, Homily Preached on 5 December 1977.
8   From the Rite of Christian Initiation of Adults: Third Scrutiny.

'AMEN!'

Like most of our prayers, the Creed of the Church ends with the Hebrew word 'Amen'. The Lord himself often used the word to emphasise the trustworthiness of his teaching and his authority founded on God's truth.

The Creed's final 'Amen' repeats and confirms all the content of our faith that has gone before. To say 'Amen' is to entrust oneself completely to him who is the 'Amen' of infinite love and perfect faithfulness. It is a deep and profound way of saying 'so be it' to the things that God has revealed and our absorption into the mystery of God's love.

The Lord Jesus himself is the great 'Amen' of the Father's love for us. He takes up and completes our 'Amen' to the Father, 'For all the promises of God find their Yes in him. That is why we utter the "Amen" through him, to the glory of God' (2 Corinthians 1:20).

Prayer:

'Through him, with him, in him,
in the unity of the Holy Spirit,
All glory and honour is yours almighty Father,
for ever and ever. AMEN!'

Conclusion

There is a beautiful prayer in the rite of baptism that the priest or deacon makes on behalf of those gathered. It is made after we have publicly professed the faith of the Apostles as contained in the creed: 'This is our faith, this is the faith of the Church and we are proud to profess it in Christ Jesus Our Lord'. Let us not only be proud but also grateful to God who has blessed us with the gift and treasure that is our faith. Let us remember that without his love we would not enjoy this gift for it is love that makes faith, not faith love.

In the words of St Augustine we conclude our reflections in the joy of being able to stand together with our fellow Christians and speak from our hearts, 'I believe ...'.

'May your Creed be for you as a mirror. Look at yourself in it, to see if you believe everything you say you believe. And rejoice in your faith every day'.[1]

Closing Prayer:

'I will rejoice at my tribulations and infirmities and be strong in the Lord, at all times giving thanks to God the Father and to his only Son our Lord Jesus Christ and to the Holy Spirit, for the great grace he has given me in deigning to assure me, his unworthy servant, while I am still alive, that his kingdom will be mine.'[2]

---

1 St Augustine, *Sermon* 58, II, 13.
2 Francis of Assisi, 'Mirror of Perfection C', *The Prayers of Saint Francis*, W. Bader (ed.), New York: New City Press, 1988.